EXPENDABLE

OTHER BOOKS OF BARRY BLACKSTONE

Though None Go With Me
Rendezvous in Paris
Though One Go With Me
Scotland Journey
The Region Beyond
Enlarge My Coast
From Dan to Beersheba and Beyond
The Uttermost Part
Homestead Homilies
Rover: A Boy's Best Friend
North to Alaska and Back
Another Day in Nazareth
Sermonettes from the Seashore
Earth's Farthest Bounds
Angling Admonitions
Beyond the Bend

EXPENDABLE

BARRY BLACKSTONE

RESOURCE *Publications* • Eugene, Oregon

EXPENDABLE

Copyright © 2021 Barry Blackstone. All rights reserved. Except for brief quotations in critical publications or reviews, no part of this book may be reproduced in any manner without prior written permission from the publisher. Write: Permissions, Wipf and Stock Publishers, 199 W. 8th Ave., Suite 3, Eugene, OR 97401.

Resource Publications
An Imprint of Wipf and Stock Publishers
199 W. 8th Ave., Suite 3
Eugene, OR 97401

www.wipfandstock.com

PAPERBACK ISBN: 978-1-6667-1712-9
HARDCOVER ISBN: 978-1-6667-1713-6
EBOOK ISBN: 978-1-6667-1714-3

. DECEMBER 16, 2021 8:15 AM

I dedicate this series of biblical biographies to the memory of my Uncle Ben (Benjamin Stanely Barton) who inspired this book project because of his willingness to make the greatest sacrifice in the service of our Lord and Saviour Jesus Christ.

TABLE OF CONTENTS

Prelude | xi

1. Josiah—The Megiddo Martyr | 1
2. Stephen—The Dedicated Deacon | 5
3. Abel—The Blessed Brother | 9
4. Amos—The Sacrificing Shepherd | 13
5. Benjamin—The Surviving Son | 17
6. Asahel—The Wounded Warrior | 21
7. Aquila—The Exiled Evangelist | 25
8. Zebedee—The Faithful Father | 29
9. Zacharias—The Privileged Priest | 33
10. Isaac—The Sacrificial Son | 37
11. Isaiah—The Pierced Prophet | 41
12. James—The Disposable Disciple | 45
13. Lazarus—The Beloved Brother | 49
14. Samson—The Strongman Slave | 53
15. Joseph—The Stunned Stepfather | 57
16. Philemon—The Beloved Brethren | 61
17. Enoch—The Translated Type | 65

18	Ishmael—The Troubled Teenager | 69
19	Ezekiel—The Priest Prophet | 73
20	John—The Great "Greatest" | 77
21	Joshua—The Soldier Shepherd | 81
22	Epaphroditus—The Courier Companion | 85
23	Jarius—The Requesting Ruler | 89
24	Nadab—The Disqualified Duo | 93
25	Lazarus—The Blessed Beggar | 97
26	Eutychus—The Saved Sleeper | 101
27	Goliath—The Great Giant | 105
28	Adam—The Immanuel Image | 109
29	Elimelech—The Famine Father | 113
30	Malchus—The Sliced Servant | 117
31	Mephibosheth—The Accepted Accident | 120
32	Hophni/Phinehas—The Scandalous Sons | 124
33	Jephthah—The Dangerous Dad | 128
34	Manoah—The Prodigal's Parent | 132
35	Barak—The Scared Soldier | 136
36	Jeremiah—The Tired Teacher | 140
37	Abner—The Treacherous Traitor | 144
38	Methuselah—The Prophetic Patriarch | 148
39	Matthew—The Accountant Apostle | 152
40	Abishai—The Cooperative Commander | 156
41	Reuben—The Burdensome Boy | 160
42	Daniel—The Supplicating Statesman | 164

43	Jonah—The Reluctant Reverend | 168
44	Elisha—The Conquering Corpse | 172
45	Gideon—The Fleece Fighter | 176
46	Tabitha—The Special Seamstress | 180
47	Abiathar—The Sole Survivor | 184
48	Mebunnai—The Tremendous Trooper | 188
49	Nathan—The Straightforward Seer | 192
50	Esau—The Despising Delinquent | 196
	Postlude | 200

PRELUDE

Revelation 12:11
...and they loved not their lives unto death.

In 1934, Vance Havner wrote his first devotional book entitled "By the Still Waters". One of the articles in that devotional book that inspired me was titled: **"When the Good Die Young"**! He first asks the soul-stirring question that has bothered many people for many centuries, including me today. Vance purposed the question in this format: "Why does God take such a useful young man, when He needs preachers so much, and when there are so many worthless characters hanging around who ought to die? It is a strange providence. It looks more like pure chance and happens-so!"

Who of us hasn't thought the same thing when we learn of the death of a young believe with such potential when a fellow believer lives on to wreck his testimony, the reputation of the local church, and the cause of Christ. Before Havner finishes his chapter he gives this interesting answer to his own question: "God is not so much interested in how long we live, or how much we do, as in our willingness to do! The supreme thing in life is not the amount of work done: it is not how many sermons have been preached, nor how many songs sung, or good deeds done. It is a matter of whether we are willing to do as long as we can. With some, God gives them a long time to prove willingness to work. With others, He accepts the will for the deed and carries them on into the next world to serve Him there." What I believe Vance Havner was writing about and what the Bible teaches very clearly is that many of God's servants are "expendable" when it comes to God working out His perfect will and divine plan. There remains this question, however: Am I willing to be 'expendable' as a man like Jim Elliot was?

PRELUDE

For years, I too have pondered the significance of those that **'loved not their lives unto death'**; those who willingly exchanged life for death; seemingly sometimes so cheaply. Granted, some have died the martyr's death as glorious as Stephen's departure (Acts 7), but what of those who have died so young in the service of the King from say a sickness? Inspired by my own spiritual heritage would you permit me to share a tiny bit from my family's history that will I hope highlight and underline the theme of this book:

"Benjamin Stanley Barton was born on October 9, 1895, an older brother of my grandfather Barton, my mother's father. Benjamin spent his early life between school and farm work. In March 1918, he received his diploma from Houlton Business College in Maine. On July 25, 1918, he enlisted in the United States Army and served as a private in the 36th Machine Gun Battalion of the 12th Division, receiving an honorable discharge on January 21, 1919 after the ending of the First World War. Returning to his hometown of Hodgdon, Maine, Benjamin continued his studies and was actively involved in his home church, the Union Church of East Hodgdon, where he had been 'born again' and baptized in the summer of 1914. It was during special meetings in the winter of 1920 that Uncle Ben yielded his life to full-time Christian service as a missionary. In 1921, Benjamin entered the Christian and Missionary Alliance Training School in Nyack, New York. Upon graduation in 1924, he was sent out as a "missionary colporteur"-a person who goes from place to place distributing Bibles, into the Canadian Northwest. He served the Lord in that capacity until he got a call from the Foreign Mission Board; having been accepted as one of their out-going missionaries for a pioneer work in Peru, South America. <u>**"His heart had been enlarged"**</u> (Psalm 119:32) to include the native peoples of Peru. As to the year and a half of the time he spend in that work a co-worker wrote this of him: "You will have today in all possibility received my cable stating the sad fact of Brother Barton having to return home with active tuberculosis. We feel more than we could possibly express for our brother personally, and can only commit him to God, and trust before long he may return and fill his place in the jungle party in Peru; a place will always be kept open for him! As to the loss to the party occasioned by his leaving us, I personally feel that the base and bulwark of the party, from the human side, has been levered out of place and that as a party we shall have to go on our way crippled by his absence. His life of devotion and faithfulness, and especially in the realm of prayer, will always be an inspiration and example to us as we go our way toward the problems of the forest."

PRELUDE

Uncle Ben died at 2:45 PM on July 10, 1926 in a New York Hospital on his way home to Maine at the tender age of 30!

(Postscript: just a few years ago my home church (Perham Baptist) sent out a short-term's missions group to help at a mountain mission in Peru. To the surprise of a friend on that trip they discovered a building dedicated to the memory of Benjamin Stanley Barton. It seems Uncle Ben's legacy is still living on nearly 90 years after his death and the short 18 months he actually worked on that mission field!)

The chronicles of Biblical history are filled with stories like Uncle Ben's. It is my purpose to record some of these unknown but well-known casualties in the great spiritual warfare that has been raging since we lost Abel, the patron saint of the **'expendables'**! I do not know how old Abel was when he was slain by the hands of his brother Cain, but I suspect he was very young in comparison to how old they lived in those days (check out Genesis 5). The testimony of Able is recorded by Paul with these words: "By faith Abel offered unto God a more excellent sacrifice than Cain, by which he obtained witness that he was righteous, God testifying of his gifts: and by it he being dead yet speaketh." (Hebrews 13:4) Fanny Crosby has long since met her Saviour 'face to face', yet her songs are still blessing souls to this day! Hudson Taylor has long since taken his last steps in China, yet his passion for souls still lingers in that far off and distant land in missionaries like a young lady from our church named Alison Chamberland to this day! Charles Spurgeon has long since written his last line and preached his last sermon, yet his challenges are still motivating preachers and writers like me to this day. Part of immortality, I believe, is not only living eternally in eternity, but living on in the lives of the people we have affected, helped, inspired, and have made a difference in their lives while we were alive; even if our time was short, even if it was a year and a half, a sudden meeting, an inspiring line, or one kind deed!

In William Shakespeare's famous play Henry VI, he penned this simple but amazing phrase: ". . . **too famous to live long** . . . " Over the portal to a special room that celebrates those that died young in the Hall of the Faithful in Heaven is found, I believe, this superscription: **"EXPENDABLE"**! I would like to share with you some of the Biblical portraits that are hanging from those celestial walls!

Barry Blackstone
June 2001

1

Josiah—The Megiddo Martyr

II Kings 23:29-30

In his days Pharaoh-Nechoh king of Egypt went up against the king of Assyria to the river Euphrates: and King Josiah went against him; and he slew him at Megiddo, when he had seen him. And his servants carried him in a chariot dead from Megiddo, and brought him to Jerusalem, and buried him in his own sepulchre.

JUDAH HAD FALLEN INTO DEEP religious depravity during the long and terrible reign of Josiah's grandfather, Manasseh. Despite Manasseh's conversion later in life (II Chronicles 33:10-13) and his attempts to undo the evil he had afflicted on the nation (II Chronicles 33:14-17), he died leaving the kingdom in the care of his wicked son Amon, Josiah's father (II Kings 21:19-22). However, just two years after Josiah's grandfather's death his father Amon was murdered. Josiah was only eight years old when his tiny hands were wrapped around the scepter of Judah (II Kings 22:1)!

Though very young, Josiah showed a trueness to God: "... and he did that which was right in the sight of the Lord and walked in all the way of David his father, and turned not aside to the right hand or to the left." (II Kings 22:2) When Josiah was sixteen (II Chronicles 34:3), he launched a spiritual reformation unprecedented in the history of his nation. Singlehanded, he cleaned up Judaism of all its pagan rituals. Throughout the land the pagan shrines were destroyed, the old Levitical worship system was reinstituted, and the temple of the Living God in Jerusalem was purified. Josiah seemed to be the man of his age, a David, a Solomon, a rare and valuable servant to the Almighty God, or was he?

When Josiah was 26, he began the long overdue repairs to the Temple of God (II Chronicles 34:8), and in so doing found a lost copy of the Mosaic Law in the rubble! When the book was read to the King he " . . . **rent his cloths . . .** " (II Chronicles 34:19) in horror of just how far the people of God had turned from their God and just how far they had slipped away from living the way Jehovah wanted them to live. "And Josiah took away all the abominations out of all the countries that pertained to the children of Israel and made all that were present in Israel to serve, even to serve the Lord their God. And all his days they departed not from following the Lord, the God of their fathers." (II Chronicles 34:33) And yet, at the height of Josiah's influence and reform of Israel, he was permitted to die on a battlefield fighting a war that he shouldn't have even been fighting in, and he was only 39 years old! (I know of 39 year olds dying, for my only son Scott died in a fight with lung and liver cancer at that very same age.)

Politically, the region was changing as fast as Josiah's religious reforms. The Assyrian Empire was crumbling after their magnificent capital of Nineveh was destroyed in 612 BC by Babylon, the new bully-on-the-block. Josiah, inspired by God, even carried his reforms to the old kingdom of Israel, better known as the Northern Kingdom, and had extended his influence as far north as Galilee, and west to the Mediterranean Sea. However, Pharaoh-Nechoh of Egypt had other plans. Realizing the growing threat of Babylon, he decided to march north in aid of the Assyrians to preserve the buffer zone between Egypt and Babylon. (II Chronicles 35:20) Pharaoh knew that once Babylon had conquered the Middle East Egypt would be next (Eventually, Babylon would conquer Egypt.) However, Josiah saw the advance of Egypt as a threat to his new found religious and political freedom. So Josiah mustered his army and about 50 miles northwest of Jerusalem, at a place called Megiddo, he tried to stop the Egyptian advance!

In 2010, I had the privilege to visit the battlefield of Megiddo and discover why so many military battles had been fought there. This hill and surrounding plains guards 'the way of the sea' better known as the Via Maris: the main trade route and highway of the Middle East in the old days. If you were travelling in the days of Josiah between Egypt and Assyria this would be the easiest and best route to take. Nechoh sought at first just to go through. He seemingly had no aspiration to interfere with Josiah's reform;

he just wanted to help his alley on the Euphrates River. (II Chronicles 35:20) To fight with Josiah would delay his trip and weaken his army, so Nechoh tried to negotiate his way through but Josiah would have nothing to do with a diplomatic solution, for Josiah was in a mood for a fight. "Josiah, however, would not turn away from him, but disguised himself to engage him in battle. He would not listen to what Nechoh had said (II Chronicles 35:21) at God's command but went to fight him on the plains of Megiddo." (II Chronicles 35:22) Josiah's sacrifice did weaken Pharaoh's army and he would eventually lose at the Battle of Carchemish (one of the turning point battles of military history) to Nebuchadnezzar; the up and coming military genius of his day. Daniel would tell the rest of this story in his classic book by the same name, but what was the purpose of God to have his "best man" killed so early in life?

The Battle of Megiddo that claimed the life of Judah's young king was a classic mistake of man, but part of a divine plan of God. I have read and studied for years the story of Jim Elliot and his four friends. I imagine the sudden and unexpected death of Josiah shocked Judah just like the sudden and unexpected death of Jim Elliot, Nate Saint, Rogar Youderian, Ed McCully, and Peter Fleming in the jungles of Ecuador in 1956 shocked America. Their story is also a story of expendability. Some would still call it a waste of spiritual talent, godly dedication, and valuable youthfulness. Why God would allow his young king, his godly king, the best king in decades to be taken in battle? Why would God allows five of his most promising missionaries be taken in a battle against a stone-age people? All six men were cut down in the prime of their lives. All in their thirties, the answer to this thought-provoking question might be answered in the song the Ecuador Five sang on the very day of their death: "We rest in Thee, our shield and our defender. Thine is the battle. Thine shall be the praise. When we pass through the gate of pearly splendor, victors we rest with Thee through endless days." I have come to believe like with Josiah they saw themselves as expendable in the service of God. Historians say Josiah lost the Battle of Megiddo, just like the world says that the Ecuador Five lost the battle of Palm Beach, but they each entered heaven a victor, not a victim!

Am I expendable? (Romans 8:32) In the blood of the five young men, the Auca people were brought to a saving knowledge of Christ through the families of those that followed Jim, Nate, Rogar, Ed, and Peter. Just this last week I had a lady in my church who will be returning in a few weeks to teach at a Bible Institute that includes Auca students. It is important that we keep singing: "Give of your best to the Master, give of the strength of thy youth, throw your soul's flesh, glowing ardor into the battle for truth." In a war, Josiah didn't have to fight, the young king was killed, but his death worked together for 'good' (Romans 8:28): God's master plan for history. Wouldn't you be willing to be sacrificed if it meant the salvation of others, the fulfillment of God plan of the ages? The question still remains: am I expendable? Are you expendable?

2

STEPHEN—THE DEDICATED DEACON

ACTS 7:59-60

> And they stoned Stephen, calling upon God, and saying, Lord Jesus, receive my spirit. And he knelled down, and cried with a loud voice, Lord; lay not this sin to their charge. And when he had said this, he fell asleep.

NOT TOO MANY PEOPLE CAN claim to be the first at something. Some men dedicate their entire lives trying to be the first to accomplish something that has never been done before: climbing a mountain, sailing a sea, running a race; only to be recognized as being 'the first' because once it has been done once somebody will do it twice! The Bible character we are highlighting in this chapter on 'expendable' is one of those rare individuals who were 'the first' even if he didn't try to be. His name was Stephen and he became known as the first martyr of the early Church. There would be scores to follow him (as I write this article (2017) has just rolled around and in so doing the "Voice of the Martyrs" has just put out a sobering statistic for 2016: nearly 10,000 people around the world gave their lives last year for the Cause of Christ!), but Stephen will always be considered 'the first'. Even this dynamic, dedicated, devote deacon of the Church was 'expendable' in God's service!

During the 1980s, I ministered at a church on the coast of Maine (actually an island off the downeast coast of Maine) that had been in existence since 1792! One of the things I did while I was there was try to write a brief history of the historic assembly (a church that is now 225 years old at this writing) that was printed in a bi-monthly newsletter we put together to keep the people of the church informed. It was an attempt on my part to show the people of their church their spiritual roots. One of the areas of consideration was the leadership of the Washington Street Baptist Church; the string of men and women that had held the church together all those years. Paul called such people: " ... pillars ... " (Galatians 2:9) The church in Eastport, Maine had many pillars, but there has to be a first and there was. Solomon Mabee was the first appointed deacon of Washington Street, but Stephen was the first appointed deacon of the Church (Acts 6:5).

In the early days of the Church in Jerusalem, a dispute had risen over the daily allotment of food for the widows (Acts 6:1). To handle the situation, the original Apostles suggested to the general Church body that they choose out from among themselves certain men to put in charge of overseeing this situation, so that they might be able to continue with their primary responsibilities in the Church (Acts 6:2–4). The Church liked the idea (a point I love to make is the early leadership were not spiritual dictators, but they actively got the Church body involved in the affairs of the Church) and there after instituted the office of deacon (Philippians 1:1). How sad that the office has gotten away from its original intent. Widows still need deacons today, but the office of deacon has taken on so many other responsibilities to the neglect of their primary purpose! In my nearly fifty years in the pastorate I have ministered with nearly 50 men called to be deacons, but very few have ever fulfilled the office as the early Church instructed. Yes, in my opinion there have been few Stephens, but there have been some and one of the best in my belief was a deacon of the Washington Street Baptist and his name was Fred Boone! A few years back I wrote this about this deacon extraordinary: Call him a custodian, a janitor, a caretaker, and a sexton-whatever; Fred was an odd-job specialist. He kept all the machinery working, from the furnace to the fixtures. He was an electrician, a plumber, a painter, and a gardener. A product of Moose Island, Fred took an early retirement from a Pratt/Whitney plant in Connecticut to return home to take care of a dying widow; his mother and the Washington Street Baptist Church widows, his seaside firmament. Handyman Fred mowed the lawn, found lost articles left by the Sunday school kids, repaired the furniture, cleaned up after suppers, oiled squeaky doors (and there plenty of them in the 150-year old building), helped in the kitchen at all function, filled the baptistery, fixed the roof when it leaked and repaired the walls when they cracked. Much of what Mr. Boone did was not under his job description, but he did them anyway. Fred was one of those church members as Washington Street, I found hard to define what department he was in, for at times he seemed to be in them all. He loved the Lord and he loved the church and he really loved the widows of the Body of Christ! Fred's was always about a 'work of faith' and a 'labor of love'. Oh, the church had a pastor, that was me, a deacon board and a trustee board, Sunday school department, a social committee, and youth leaders, but despite these well-meaning helpers, the services of the church and the programs of the assembly would have ground to a halt if not for Mr. Fix-It. No one knew he was around most of the time, for he was never self-imposing, but when you needed something, needed some help Fred was there whether at church or at the home of the local widow fixing things for them. When I think back to the passing of this deacon into glory a number of years ago I realize Fred was a Stephen and the widows of Eastport were graced to have had him for as long as they did!

I will meet Stephen one day, but until then I will see his ministry through the exploits of Fred Boone because when I read of this amazing man's qualification for the first position of deacon they remind me of Fred. Stephen was known as a man 'full of faith and power' and 'he did great wonders and miracles among the people.' (Acts 6:8) Stephen first fulfilled his obligation to serve the church; that is what deacon means 'servant'! However, Stephen didn't stop there, for he also realized that the Great Commission wasn't just for the Apostles (Matthew 28:19–20), so he also spread the Word. Fred was also a great soul winner, evangelist (II Timothy 4:5); though he would have never considered himself one. How often I have heard that is the pastor's job, but men like Stephen and Fred didn't believe that. One of the first deacons I had in a small pioneer work in New Hampshire is now a pastor in South Carolina, a real Stephen.

But Stephen's call to fame in the early Church wasn't his deaconship, or his preaching, but in how he died. It is in this category I ask the question again: Why God would allow his top deacon, one of the best of the first generation of church members to be martyred by stoning. I have come to believe that God needed to get the Church moving into the second phase of the great Commission. I believe the early Church got content with Jerusalem and they forgot about Judaea and Samaria (Acts 1:8). Have you ever noticed after Stephen's death it says: " . . . . .they were all scattered aboard throughout the regions of Judaea and Samaria . . . . ." (Acts 8:1) The catalyst for this expansion of the Church was the death of Stephen (Acts 11:19). Stephen was used of God to help the widows, spread the Word, and restart the Church on its path to going to 'the uttermost parts of the earth'! Stephen was faithful in life and he was 'faithful unto death' (Revelation 2:10), a fitting memorial to the Church's first deacon and first martyr. You might never be the first in anything you do, but you can still be called one of the 'finest' if you do whatsoever, wheresoever the Good Lord has called you. Dedicated, devoted to the Cause of Christ whether in the short term (expendable) or in a long term ministry!

3

Abel—The Blessed Brother

Hebrews 11:4

By faith Able offered unto God a more excellent sacrifice than Cain, by which he obtained witness that he was righteous, God testifying of his gifts: and by it he being dead yet speaketh.

WE HAVE BEEN TRYING TO highlight and underlines a Biblical concept that few recognize. I have come to the belief that 'expendable' is one of the first precepts given in Holy Writ through the story of Abel. When Paul makes a listing of " . . . the elders who obtained a good report . . . " (Hebrews 11:2) he starts with the 4th person to inhabit this planet. I find it interesting that Paul didn't start with Adam or Eve, but they are distinctly missing from the list. I have come to believe that they are not listed because of their sin in the Garden of Eden (Genesis 3). It was Paul's opinion, supported by the Spirit (II Peter 1:21) that Abel was the first person to **'walk by faith and not by sight'** (II Corinthians 5:7). Granted, I do believe that Paul primary purpose for Hebrews 11 was to fortify the classic doctrine: "The Just Shall Live By Faith" (Hebrews 10:38, Romans 1:17, Galatians 3:11, and Habakkuk 2:4). But as you know by now I have also come to believe Abel is another great example of how God often sacrificed the best of the best and leaves the worst of the worst to live. Even Abel was expendable in the master plan of God for the ages.

Expendable

Abel lived in direct contrast to the depraved nature passed on to both he and his older brother Cain. "Wherefore, as by one man sin entered into the world and death by sin." (Romans 5:12) Abel would become the first person to feel the full fury of sin, not because he was a great sinner (for he did sin-Romans 3:23), but because of the great sinner he lived with. Unlike his father, his mother, and his brother who all died by the old age process of sin: "and all the days of Adam loved were nine hundred and thirty years, and he died." (Genesis 5:5) Abel would be the first of millions to die a violent and terrible death; a death by the hands of his own brother. As you go through the Bible and find the 'expendable', you will find this often the case: Josiah and Stephen are our two examples so far. We have yet to talk of Naboth whose faithfulness to his ancestral land resulted in his being stoned to death (I Kings 21). Remember John the Baptist whose faithfulness to the commands of God against adultery in marriage resulted in him being beheaded (Matthew 14). Remember James the apostle who faithfulness to the preaching of the Gospel of Christ resulted in a death by a sword (Acts 12). I have come to believe that Abel was the patron saint to all these expendable ones; men and women that were " . . . faithful unto death . . . " (Revelation 2:10) In the town of Pergamos there was such a man" " . . . Even in those days where in Antipas was a faithful martyr, who was slain among you . . . " (Revelation 2:13) I have often thought that Abel and Antipas are the Scriptural book ends of this Biblical topic of "Expendable"!

Yet we read: " . . . and by it he being dead yet speaketh . . . " I have come to believe that this might just be the first reason of the expendable: that in their death there is a greater platform for a message to be delivered. I believe what Paul was referring to is what God said to Cain on the day that he murdered his bother: "What hast thou done? The voice of they brother's blood crieth unto me from the ground." (Genesis 4:10) He could have been referring to the fact that Abel's faithfulness was still being remembered even as Christ said: " . . . that upon you may come all the righteous blood shed upon the earth from the blood of righteous Abel unto . . . " (Matthew 23:35) Whatever the message the facts are clear and that being that Abel was the first recorded man to worship God according to the command of substitutionary sacrifice; thereby placing his belief in the coming sacrifice of our Lord and Saviour Jesus Christ. His worship brought a violent response from the more liberal worshipper Cain who sought to worship Jehovah through a works kind of faith, a self-fulfilling worship that highlighted and underlined what the worshiper had done verses what the worshipped

Abel—The Blessed Brother

would do! Abel's faith was worth dying for and has been since the days of Abel fulfilling one of Christ's predictions: "And the brother shall deliver up the brother to death . . . " (Matthew 10:21)

I don't know what we'll do in America when we lose the last true Christian. Call him a believer, a Christian, a follower of the way-what you will, but if we lose the old fashion faithful saint we're lost. It is the Christian who is keeping the prayer pipeline filled to the throne of grace (Hebrews 4:16), and for me it is the unsung, unrecognized, and unrewarded hero of this land. For if it were not for the family of God, America's prosperity would and could never have happened. Abel is still speaking today after all these years and this is what he is saying to me. It is this speaking that for me is the reason for his expendability: As I look back now with perfect twenty/twenty Biblical vision and hindsight. I see that Abel came into the first family to fulfill a role that nobody else could ever fulfill; all a part of God's master plan. Despite being the second born son to Adam and Eve (Genesis 4:1-2) Abel was not a farmer, no Gardner like his father and brother. His brother followed in the footsteps of Adam, a plowman, a farm hand, a sharecropper at best, a man that trusted in his hands, his work ethic. Abel on the other hand found that in raising sheep he was closer to God; had to trust God more. Over time, how much time, how old was Abel, Abel become the real 'man of God' in the family; the one that took up the belief that not by the works of the hand, but by the blood of the lamb a man could be found 'righteous'. Abel became the spiritual man and Cain became the natural man as Paul describes them in I Corinthians 2:13-15.

So Abel believed in the blood and Cain came to believe in beans and beets and barley and anything else he could produce with his hard work and hands. In the end it was this clash of beliefs that brought the infamous first killing (Genesis 4:8). What so many fail to see is that God came to Cain and warned him of the evil intent of his heart (Genesis 4:6-7). A failure to listen resulted in the first murder (I John 3:12). I feel it came down to the love of Saviour verses the love of self. Cain would become the prototype of mankind and their constant attempt to justify themselves verses those that believe: "for by grace are ye saved through faith; and that not of yourselves: it is the gift of God; not of works, lest any man should boast." (Ephesians 2:8-9) I believe Cain sought a man-made sacrifice verses the God-made sacrifice of Abel. It was Abel act of a blood sacrifice that resulted in him being called 'righteous'. In the Old Testament it was the acts of the men and women of faith that made this possible; like with Abraham: "And he believed in the Lord; and he was counted it to him for righteousness." (Genesis 15:6) It is a walk of faith with God verses walking alone with a mark (Genesis 4:15)

Abel was the first martyr for a particular kind of faith, a faith that would reach down through the ages to every generation; a faith in the sacrificial sacrifice of Christ verses the sacrificial sacrifice of man (Genesis 4:3–4); which would God choice (Genesis 4:5), and why? Because it best represented the kind of sacrifice His Son would ultimately make on Calvary's tree. Abel spoke of it first even though he had to do it through demonstrating the kind of death that Jesus would have to suffer (Philippians 2:8). Both Expendable!

4

Amos—The Sacrificing Shepherd

Amos 7:14–15

> Then answered Amos, and said to Amaziah, I was no prophet, neither was I a prophet's son; but I was a herdman, and gatherer of sycamore fruit: and the Lord took me as I followed the flock, and the Lord said unto me, Go, prophesy unto my people Israel.

Everybody should have, surely needs an Amos in their lives, in their living, and in their lifestyle! If you are fortunate like I have been, then your life has been blessed with an Amos. If not, then you are still wandering around helpless and aimless in search for someone, anybody who is willing to sacrifice his or her career that your life maybe enriched, fortified, and meaningful. When it comes to being 'expendable', sometimes the Lord doesn't ask you to lay down your life like he did with Abel, Stephen, and Josiah, He simply asks you to sacrifice your dreams and desires for another course, another direction just like He did when He called Amos!

Amos was one of God's prophets during the 8th century BC. Today we call him a 'minor prophet' because of the length of his book, but I hope before you finish reading this chapter you will see him in the light of an Isaiah, a Jeremiah, an Ezekiel, or a Daniel! What made Amos unique was his background; he didn't come from a prophet's family, or a prophet's school. He was not of the priestly class or the princely class. Amos was a simple shepherd and a sycamore tree dresser from the village of Tekoa, just south of Bethlehem. When I think of Amos I am always reminded of who Jesus called to be His disciples. One of the best descriptions I have found on the disciples is the words from the elite of their day: " . . . .and perceived that they were unlearned and ignorant men . . . ." (Acts 4:13) That was Amos! I also thought of this question asked by Nathaniel when Philip suggested to him that he had found the Messiah: "Can there any good thing come out of Nazareth?" (John 1:46) I suspect that Amos got that a lot as his name began to appear in the mouths of those who thought that he was just a yokel from the sticks. This image of the prophet really came to light when he travelled to Bethel, the so called religious center of Israel. Amos was kind of rough. He was no preacher. He hadn't been to Bible school. He didn't have any 'letters' behind his name. Prophesy was not his profession. He had no parentage behind him. His only called was providence and he would prove to be a nonconformist, an unregimented, and unclassified. He was unique, unusual, and peculiar to say the least, but he was God's man for the time. So why would anybody leave the quiet of the country life, the solitude of the shepherd's life for a city-ministry? When I made such a move (I came from a very small town in Northern Maine, but most of my time as a pastor has been in the bigger towns and larger cities of Maine). When I fought the change the Good Lord directed my attention to this poem by George McDonald I found in Mrs. Charles E. Cowan's book "Springs in the Valley": "I said, Let me walk in the fields. He said, No walk in the town. I said, there are no flowers there. He said, No flowers but a crown. I said, but the skies are black; there is nothing but noise and din! And He wept as He sent me back, there is more, He said, there is sin. I said, but the air is thick, and fogs are veiling the sun. He answered; ye souls are sick and souls in the darkness undone. I said, I shall miss the light, and friends will miss me, they say. He answered, Choose tonight. If I am to miss you or they? I pleaded for time to be given. He said, is it hard to decide? It will not seem hard in heaven to have followed the steps of your Guide! I cast one look at the fields, and then set my face to the town. He said my child do you yield? Will you leave the flowers for a crown? Then into His hand went mine, and into my heart came he. And I walked in a light divine, the path I feared to see!" I have wondered if Amos had a similar encounter with the Lord before Bethel in Tekoa.

    Amos had been moved by God to make a pilgrimage to Bethel to denounce the idolatrous worship going on there by Northern Israel. Bethel, along with Dan, had become the national shrine of the apostate faith of the nation when ten tribes split with their southern cousins. Amos' blunt condemnation of the social and spiritual sins of the nation brought accusations of treason by Amaziah, the high priest of Bethel. Despite being ordered out of Bethel, Amos continued to warn the people of the impending judgment of God upon the tribes, if they didn't repent of their gross transgressions and evil iniquities. Using one of the most graphic images of the Bible, the famous basket of fruit (Amos 8) and the plumb line (Amos 7), Amos illustrates his messages of warning and woe. Then as suddenly as he came on the world stage Amos disappears probably to return to Tekoa and to write his wonderful book that is still read and studied to this day.

For me, Amos was my father, Wendell E. Blackstone, dairy and potato farm extra ordinary. In 1984, I paid homage to my father with these few lines on his 60th birthday (at the time of this rewrite of 'expendable' Dad is nearing 93!): The years have passed and the picture I have of my Dad has now become much clearer. I remember Dad as a demonstrator, not a dictator; a quiet man who spoke little, but taught much. It has only been in these latter years that I have realized just how much of his teaching has shaped my life. He taught me how to pray, by praying. Never a meal went by without him bowing his head in prayer, potato house or farm house. Never a night went by, but I found him not on his knees kneeling by his bed in prayer. Never a Wednesday night, planting or harvesting, did I not find him at the mid-week prayer meeting of the Perham Baptist Church. Is that why I cannot understand why Christians do not have time for prayer? Is that why I accept no excuse for anyone missing the prayer meeting on Wednesday, no matter the business? Is that why I believe that prayer is the essential tenet of our Faith? He taught me to 'be there', by being there. He was there when my dog Rover was hit by a passing car, and he made it alright and understandable. He was there when I lost my only tournament basketball game at the Bangor Auditorium, and he said the right thing: "It's only a game!" And he was right, it was only a game. He was there when I called from New Hampshire in financial trouble, and he had the right advice, and a helpful check. He was there when I was struggling in my calling to pastor my home church with his full support and backing despite the fact the church rejected my application! Is that why when others are in need I want, I need to 'be there'! Is that why when someone calls I go no matter the time or the trouble? Is that when someone needs someone I must be the one? Little did I know the example my father set for me, and it wasn't until late in life I finally heard the story how Dad after the Second World War, in which he served in Italy, forsook his desire to go to college, go into sport's medicine, but instead came home to farm with his father and be a pattern for me. Is that why I didn't find it hard to give up my dreams of being a history teacher to become a pastor because like my Dad the Good Lord called us to something different than we dreamed!

Like Amos, Dad was willing to become whatever the Almighty wanted him to be. Sometimes the Lord asks us to make our wishes and our wants 'expendable' to His will. What my Dad found out, as I have found out, and I believe Amos found out, is that when you chose God's path for your life, something's are expendable, but in the end profitable!

5

BENJAMIN—THE SURVIVING SON

GENESIS 43:14

And God Almighty give you mercy before the man, that he may send away your other brother, and Benjamin. If I be bereaved of my children, I am bereaved.

IT HAS SATISFIED MY SPIRITUAL APPETITE and inspired these articles the more I pondered who I would use as an example of 'expendable' that old familiar stories learned in my childhood at Sunday school contain an element of expendability in them. Until I had set my mind on this series of devotionals I had missed so many acts of sacrifice in the "God-breathed" (II Timothy 3:16) stories of the Bible. Take for an example the hero of this chapter. If it hadn't been for the sacrifice of his mother (Rachel-Genesis 35:16–20) this notable Old Testament character would never have lived. Benjamin owed his life to the expendability of Jacob's favorite wife. Childbirth is not only a very painful experience (Genesis 3:16); it can also be a very dangerous experience (I Samuel 4:19–22). Every time a woman gets pregnant she is risking her life, and saying: "I am expendable that my child maybe born!" I know it doesn't happen as much today as yesterday, but it still happens despite all the advancements made in the care of the expectant mothers and their children. But it is not this aspect of expendability I wish to highlight and underline in this chapter on 'expendable'. Our focus will be on the son that was born that day that Rachel died and was buried near Bethlehem.

Benjamin was the twelfth and last son born to the great patriarch Jacob, eventually called Israel. Interestingly, Benjamin was the only son of Jacob to actually be born in Canaan, the land of promise. Rachel named him "Benoni", or 'son of my sorrow' (she must have known she was dying-Genesis 35:18). Was it the sorrow of childbirth, the sorrow of dying, or the sorrow over the silly contest (Genesis 30:1) she had been waging with his sister Leah on how many 'boys' each could produce for Jacob? Upon Rachel's death Jacob would rename his youngest son "Benjamin", or 'son of my right hand'! No reason is given for this change, but for me it does bring up an amazing connection to Jesus Christ. Some even go as far to make Benjamin a type of Christ in the truth that is revealed in the New Testament that Jesus is "the Son of God's right hand"-Acts 7:56, Romans 8:34, Ephesians 1:20, Colossians 3:1, and Hebrews 1:3!

As the story of Jacob unfolds and the tragic story of Joseph develops Benjamin become the focal point of the story. I know most miss this part of the story because we are so focused on Joseph's ups and downs and Jacob as he reaps what he had sown in his early years. I have come to believe this part of Jacob's story is because Rachel had been Jacob's 'first love' (Genesis 29:18) and eventually his 'favorite wife' (he would have four). As God willed it, Rachel also become Jacob's 'first lose', followed by Joseph, and then maybe Benjamin, so the love Jacob had for Rachel and Joseph would automatically transferred to his surviving son Benjamin. It will be around this connection that our story of expendable will reemerge after twenty years with Benjamin being, as Jacob believed, his only son still remaining from his love of Benjamin's mother!

The next time Benjamin appears on the sacred record is at the height of the great famine. Jacob prepares to send his ten older sons to Egypt for food, but Benjamin would not go: " **. . . peradventure mischief befall him . . .** " (Genesis 42:4) After seemingly the untimely death of Jacob's favorite son Joseph, Jacob filled the void and grief in his life with Benjamin. Jacob had become very protective of Rachel's last boy! Despite this over protection of Benjamin, events beyond Jacob's control would bring Benjamin back into the story developing in Egypt. For upon the return of Benjamin's brothers from Egypt with enough food to keep the family alive for a while, the bad news was delivered to Jacob. Simeon was in captivity in Pharaoh's prison (Genesis 42:24) and if his sons return they must bring Benjamin (Genesis

BENJAMIN—THE SURVIVING SON

42:36). Jacob's reaction was **"All things are against me!"** He couldn't give up Benjamin; Benjamin was not expendable, or was he!

Maybe today you feel the same way. Has something or someone in your life you thought not expendable turned out to be expendable with God? Are you reeling from a loss so serious that it has changed your entire outlook on life? Life has dealt you a serious blow, a right hook, an unforeseen tragedy, yet we know in the story of Jacob that ultimately **" . . . all things will work together for good . . . "** (Romans 8:28) But can you believe that in the midst of your test? You know the story from here on out don't you? Eventually Jacob had to put Benjamin on the altar and sent him to Egypt in order to save the rest of his clan. Instead of losing a son he gained another son back in Joseph. It is important for all of us that find ourselves in these situation to wait on the Lord, to be patient and see what the Good Lord has in store because ultimately it will probably turn our much better than we dreamed, and not as worse as we dreaded. When God writes the final chapter in our lives we will realize what He asked us to sacrifice was really not expendable at all!

Despite the emotion, the roller coaster emotion Benjamin went through, we can see the parallel to the life of Christ. Consider these amazing similarities: As Benjamin had to go to a strange world (Genesis 43:15), so did Jesus (John 1:11); as Benjamin was falsely accused (Genesis 44:12), so was Jesus (Matthew 26:60), and even though Benjamin didn't have to die he was under threat of death (Genesis 44:17), so as Jesus died (Philippians 2:8). Jesus died but was eventually delivered back to the Father (Acts 1:11), just like Benjamin (Genesis 45:25-28). So often we see in the shadows of the Old Testament in the substance in the New Testament. Let us never forget that the Eternal Father saw His Son as expendable: **"He that shared not his own Son, but delivered Him up for us all . . . "** (Romans 8:32) As with the Father, Jacob finally realized that he must send Benjamin to Egypt that his family might be saved, just like in eternity past the Heavenly Father realized if the human race were to be redeemed He would have to give his only begotten Son (John 3:16)!

The last mention of Benjamin in the Scriptures is in relationship to his father's dying. As one by one the sons of Jacob came to his bedside, Israel made a prophesy about the future of each of the tribes of Jacob. From the first to the last and in the last Benjamin heard this: "Benjamin shall ravin as a wolf in the morning, he shall devour the prey and at night he shall divide the spoil." (Genesis 49:27) Twelve times the word 'wolf' is mentioned in the

Bible, and each time it speaks of 'ferocious'! (Habakkuk 1:8) Jesus likened false prophets to wolves that scatter and slaughter the flock (Matthew 7:15). When Jesus sent His disciples He said to them: "I send you . . . as sheep in the midst of wolves..." (Matthew 10:16) A study of the history of the tribe of Benjamin will reveal that the offspring of Benjamin were 'wolf-like' (Judges 20:21, 25-King Saul-I Samuel 9:1 and Ezekiel 22:27 and what of Paul-Philippians 3:5-when he was Saul and his attack on the Church of Christ was wolf-like). Maybe you are fiery, ferocious, ravenous, but there is One what can change you from a wolf to a lamb (Jeremiah 13:23-II Corinthians 5:17); this change is possible because somebody was expendable, and His name is Jesus.

6

Asahel—The Wounded Warrior

II Samuel 2:23

Howbeit he refused to turn aide: wherefore Abner with the hinder end of the spear smote him under the fifth rib, that the spear came out behind him; and he fell there, and died in the same place: and it came to pass, that as many as came to the place where Asahel fell down and died stood still.

The death of this valiant warrior, numbered among David's famous 'mighty men' (I Chronicles 11:26) took place: "Now there was long war between the house of Saul and the house of David: but David waxed stronger and stronger, and the house of Saul waxed weaker and weaker." (II Samuel 3:1) We often overlook that there was a king of Israel after the death of King Saul at the Battle of Gilboa (II Samuel 31). His name was Ishbosheth, one of the surviving sons of Saul, but the power behind the thrown was a general named Abner. For two years (II Samuel 2:8) this pair was able to hold off the claims of David to the throne (II Samuel 2:8). Through strategic maneuver and technical advantage, Abner was able to hold back the increasing advantages of David and his forces. During this Civil War, a very interesting battle took place at Gibeon between the combined forces of Ishbosheth under the commanded of Abner and the combine forces of David under the commanded of David's cousin Joab (II Samuel 2:12–17). After the initial conflict, David's forces had Abner's force on the run. One of the heroes of

Expendable

that struggle was a young warrior named Asahel (II Samuel 23:24), the son of David's sister Zeruiah (I Chronicles 2:15–16). In David's chain of command this young cousin rose to 4th (I Chronicles 27:7). No doubt Asahel fought many a battles to get David the throne of Israel, but Asahel's only call to Biblical fame come at the end of the Battle of Gibeon.

The final action in that battle is best described by these notes I found in the commentary (Zondervan Publishing House 1961) by Jamieson, Fausset, and Brown: "To gain a general's armour was deemed the greatest trophy. Asahel, ambitious of securing Abner's armour, had outstripped all other pursuers, and was fast gaining on the retreating commander. Abner, conscious of possessing more physical power, and willing that there should be 'blood' between himself and Joab, Asahel's brother, twice urges him to desist. The impetuous young soldier being deaf to the generous remonstrance, the veteran raised the pointed butt of his lance, as the modern Arabs do when pursued, and, with a sudden back-thrust, transfixed him on the spot, so that he fell, and lay weltering on his blood. But Joab and Abishai continued the pursuit by another route till sunset. On reaching a rising ground, and receiving a fresh reinforcement of some Benjamites, Abner rallied his scattered troops and earnestly appealed to Joab's better feelings to stop the further effusion of blood, which, if continued, would lead to more serious consequences-a destructive civil war. Joab, which upbraiding his opponent as the sole cause of the fray, felt the force of the appeal and led off his men; while Abner probably dreading a renewal of the attack when Joab should learn of his brother's fate, and vow fierce revenge, endeavoring, by force march, to cross the Jordan by night. On David's side the loss was only 19 men, besides Asahel. But of Ishbosheth's party there fell 360. This skirmish is exactly similar to the battles of Homeric warriors, among whom, the fight of one, the pursuit by another, and the dialogue held between them, there is vividly represented the style of ancient warfare." (II Samuel 2:25–32) One must accept that any time one goes into battle that there will be those that are 'expendable', even if that one is a brother. I would like in this article to share with you what I feel is the great lesson of the Battle of Gibeon and that being a warning against carelessness in the spiritual struggle!

Asahel, in my opinion, was a veteran warrior who should have known better than to corner a retreating general without help. Asahel let the glory of a major victory cloud his judgment, and instead of being careful, he become careless to the sudden reverse thrust of Abner's spear. The hunter quickly became the hunted, and before Asahel realized the danger he was

Asahel—The Wounded Warrior

wounded and dying. So it is with us. Paul warns: "Lest Satan should get an advantage of us: for we are not ignorant of his devices." (II Corinthians 2:11) You can't tell me Asahel hadn't learned that 'back-thrust' maneuver. Asahel must have been taught the technique of defense, yet in the heat of the pursuit and the glory of capturing or killing Abner, let down his guard opening up his chest to Abner's jab. Warriors in those days carried shields to protect them from such attacks. So it is with us. The Christian armour has been given to us (Ephesians 6:10–15), and one of the pieces of that armour is 'the shield of faith' (Ephesians 6:16) which if held high can resist any 'fiery dart'. If only Asahel would have had his shield in front of him the shield would have taken the blow and Asahel would have lived. Why are so many believing Christian soldiers (II Timothy 2:3–4) falling today? Is the armour weak? Are there flaws in the shield? No, a resounding no! The problem today can be traced back to the carelessness of the warrior. So many saints have taken their amour off, or are letting their shield droop, or still have their sword in the sheath. I believe Asahel had his sword ready for the fight. I think he thought Abner would turn and fight, but he didn't and Asahel didn't expect the attack to come from Abner's rear. So too we have an enemy that will attack where and when we least expect it. We are so focused on the goal sometimes, of running right sometimes, that we fail to keep sober and alert and vigilant (I Peter 5:8) as we should. Despite Asahel's distinct advantage (II Samuel 2:18), instead of using it to his advantage, he ran straight into Abner's spear butt. So often the Christian believing he is in no danger because of his spiritual advantages lets down his guard only to run straight into a temptation he never saw coming, a trial he is not prepared for, and instead of coming out the victor he becomes another victim of Satan's crafty strategy. We end the fight wallowing in defeat (Romans 13:14); a fight that God intended us to win (I Corinthians 10:13).

Like Asahel, we too are fighting in enemy territory. We too have " . . . set to flight the armies of the aliens . . . " (Hebrews 11:34) We too have resisted the devil and he is fleeing from us (James 4:7). It is at times like these we must place a second guard on our heart, our body and our mind. One successful battle doesn't mean the fight is over. Asahel must have thought that after Gibeon Abner would be an easy win. One easy contest doesn't mean our enemy is weak. One battle doesn't make a war. Asahel forget the dangers of fighting a fleeing foe; a cornered bear can be most dangerous. Jesus never forgot and neither should we. It is said after Jesus' great defeat of the Wicked One in the Battle of the Wilderness (Matthew

4:1–12) that Satan " . . . departed from him for a season." (Luke 4:13) The Devil came back, but Jesus was always ready for his thrusts. We too will not be safe in this world no matter how many times we resist the devil and he flees. No matter how many times we defeat him he will be back. Asahel lost in the pursuit because he was careless; he thought Abner was defeated but he wasn't. I have counseled many over time who thought their 'besetting sin' (Hebrews 12:1) was conquered; their old man (Colossians 3:9) was defeated, but they were not! Let us be constantly on the alert even in times of victory lest we be ambushed and find ourselves 'expendable'!

7

AQUILA—THE EXILED EVANGELIST

ACTS 18:2

And found a certain Jew named Aquila, born in Pontus, lately comes from Italy, with his wife Priscilla; (because that Claudius had commanded all Jews to depart from Rome :) and came unto them.

THE YEAR WAS 53 AD when a decree went out from Caesar Claudius that all Jews were to leave Rome. Roman had always had a large Jewish population, but this wasn't the first time that anti-Semitism had forced the Jewish people out of the capital of the mighty Roman Empire. This particular exodus swept up a man by the name of Aquila, originally from Pontus. Seeking a place of peace where he could continue his business of tent making (Acts 18:3) with his wife Priscilla, Aquila eventually settled in Corinth (Acts 18:1). Sometimes in the divine plan of God it isn't our lifestyle or even our life that is expendable to God, but our living space! Aquila and Priscilla learned that there home and homeland were expendable in the eyes of God. This continual series of devotionals on the men and women of the Bible that were 'expendable' to God touches on a variety of variables in this hard to explain working of God. This one is also personal in the reality that I in my walk with God was led away from home; my family home was expendable.

Six times this marvelous couple is referred to in the New Testament, but like Mary and Joseph it was after a Roman emperor's edict (Luke 2:1) that their lives were really changed for the better? For at Corinth they meet Paul. They became friends through their common trade of tent making. Every Jewish lad, no matter how well to do the family, was taught a trade. That is why Jesus become a 'carpenter' (Mark 6:3) before he become a preacher or a healer. I have come to believe it was through Aquila's trade that he actually came to know the Lord through the witness of Paul. What a testimony that ought to be to all of us. We live in a time where even most Church members think the preacher is the sole soul-winner. I don't know your occupation, but if you are a Christian you ought to be using your job to win souls to Christ. I hear it from so many that you can't speak of spiritual things at the work place. The one that came up with that lie is the Devil himself. It is the same argument I hear about kids in school sharing their faith. The Devil has seemingly over ruled the first amendment! Some of the best soul-winners in the churches I have pastored were laymen and laywomen. The best I have right now is a house-keeper who uses her time in the homes of her clients to share God's Word. Paul would later write to the Church at Corinth these words: "And labour, working with our own hands." (I Corinthians 4:12) What was he doing with those hands: making tents, and while he made tents he shared his faith! I believe the connection of these two occupations: tent making and soul winning is brought out in this verse in a letter to the Thessalonians: "For ye remember brethren our labour and travail for laboring night and day because we would not be chargeable unto any of you, we preached unto you the Gospel of God."(I Thessalonians 2:9) Paul gave Aquila and Priscilla a free gospel, no price tag, no offering taken, a gift to a fellow worker. How we need to get back to this form of evangelism today!

When Paul left Corinth, Aquila and Priscilla went with him (Acts 18:18), but when they got to Ephesus they stayed while Paul moved on. (Acts 18:19) Shortly after Paul left for ministries in Syria, a certain Jew from Alexandria, Egypt arrived in Ephesus. His name was Apollos and the Bible describes him as " . . . an eloquent man, and mighty in the Scriptures." (Acts 18:24) Apollos' problem wasn't zeal, for it says of him that he was " . . . fervent in the Spirit . . . ", or urgency, for he " . . . taught diligently the things of the Lord." (Acts 18:25) Despite this great pedigree Apollos only knew of " . . . the baptism of John." This man of God needed to understand the ways of Christ more clearly, but who would teach him?

Taking him aside, Aquila did just that (Acts 18:26). They were doing exactly what their friend Paul taught them and instructed then to follow "

... the law of Christ." (Galatians 6:1–2) This simple tent maker and his wife had turned from tent makers to truth ministers. How we need laymen and laywomen to get involved in explaining and expounding the truth of Jesus. Again Paul writes of this concept in this precept from a letter to another famous evangelist, Timothy: "And the things that thou hast heard of me among many witnesses, the same commit thou to faithful men who shall be able to teach others also." (II Timothy 2:2) Is this not exactly what Aquila and Priscilla did to Apollos?

Are you such a servant of Jesus that you can jump from the secular to the sacred whenever the need arises? Or are you like the people Paul wrote about in his letter to the Hebrews: "For when for the time ye ought to be teachers ye have need that one teach you again which be the first principles of the oracles of God, and one became such as have need of milk and not of strong meat." (Hebrews 5:12) Aquila and Priscilla were not only evangelists but teachers to Apollos though I dare say Apollos was the more knowledgeable one in reference to Holy Writ. To many Christians are still on the 'milk' diet when in reality they ought to be eating and sharing 'strong meat'!

So what does it take to leave a comfort zone existence to help others in spiritual need? Often it takes a spiritual storm to get you where you can meet someone who will share the Gospel to you. Often it take a spiritual upheaval to get you to a place where you will meet the very one God wants you to help. What happened to Aquila and Priscilla happened to the early Church (Acts 8:1–3). Sometimes our lives need to be up ended; sometimes we need to move! If we won't on our own God will make a way to move you to where you need to be; remember Jonah 1–2! To be 'expendable' in this area you must know how to 'weather a storm'. Recently my mother Phyllis sent me this: "Did you know that an eagle (Isaiah 40:31) knows when a storm is approaching long before it breaks? The eagle will fly to some high spot and wait for the winds to come. When the storm hits, it sets its wings so that the wind will pick it up and lift it above the storm. While the storm rages below, the eagle is soaring above it. The eagle does not escape the storm. It simply uses the storm to lift it higher than the storm. It rises on the winds that brings the storm. When the storms of life come upon us and all of us will experience them we can rise above them by setting our minds and our belief toward God. The storms do not have to overcome us. We can allow God's power to lift us above them. God enables us to ride the winds of the storm that bring sickness, tragedy, failure, and disappointment in our lives. We can soar above the storm. Remember, it is not the burdens of life that weigh us down, it is how we handle them."

I can't tell you for sure this is how Aquila and Priscilla handled the legislative storm that threw them out of their home; that exiled them to a strange city, but it appears to me in Luke's account of them they rode above the storm after they meet Paul in Corinth and soared above the storm helping the mighty teacher Apollos to find his way. They found that in yielding to the expendability of God's plan that they became the servants He wanted them to be where He wanted them to be and to whom He wanted them to serve!

8

Zebedee—The Faithful Father

Matthew 4:21-22

And going on from thence, He saw other two brethren, James the son of Zebedee, and John his brother, in a ship with Zebedee their father, mending their nets; and He called them. And they immediately left the ship and their father, and followed Him.

For me, father Zebedee is another unsung hero in the category of the 'expendable'. Zebedee was the silent father who one day watched and heard Jesus call his two sons, James and John, into His discipleship and he never said a word, or tried to keep his sons from following Jesus. In the topic of 'expendable', the cost of serving God can come from a myriad of directions and a multitude of costs. Sometimes it is personal, and sometimes like Zebedee it will cost you your 'pride and joy', your children. It was in this area that Zebedee was called to let go, to give up his two boys and the future of his business; all expendable in Christ's service.

Zebedee seemed to be a highly successful fisherman and business man and well-known around the Sea of Galilee. Often the mention of his two sons was in conjunction with the mention of his name (Matthew 11:2). This suggests to me that at first Zebedee was better known than his sons in the region, but we know that would soon be the reverses as it is today. I dare say that few Christians if asked who James and John's father was would say Zebedee. Marks tells us that Zebedee had hired servants (Mark 1:20) besides employing his sons in the fishing business which probably lessened the blow of the departure of James and John, but also revealing that Zebedee had an extensive business, how many boats? I have come to believe that the silence of Zebedee speaks volumes in Zebedee's approval of this decision of his boys to follow Jesus. We don't have a direct verse on Zebedee's faith, but we are told that Salome, Zebedee's wife, was a follower of the Messiah (Mark 15:40–41). The indication in this seems to suggest that the Zebedee family helped with some of the expenses of Jesus' ministry (Luke 8:1–3). Some of the commentaries I checked on believe that Zebedee was first a follower of John the Baptist (remember John was a disciple of John's before Jesus'- John 1:34–39) and then became a follower of Christ after his sons? Was Zebedee one of those like Simeon (Luke 2:25) looking for the coming of the Messiah? He like Jesus' earthly father Joseph never saw the end of Jesus' ministry that is way his wife and not himself was mentioned at the end of the gospel account? Despite remaining in the shadows I am convinced that Zebedee did play a role in Christ's great earthly work, and he is a wonderful example of 'expendable', consider this simple poem: "To some Christ's calls: leave boat and bay, and white haired Zebedee? To some the call is harder: stay and mend the nets for me!" I have often wondered which was hardest. I was the son called away from the family business (Blackstone Brothers: a dairy and potato farm in Northern Maine), and my father labored on faithfully at the plow while I was off winning souls around the world.

In Mrs. Charles E. Cowman's great devotional book of 1939, "Springs in the Valley", she records this poem called "Zebedee's Sons" which perhaps describes best the choice of Zebedee, and I quote: "Salome! Had you been with me in the boat? You would not chide and moan because our boys have gone with the Beloved from this our home. Let me, Salome, tell you how it came. The night was still-the tide was running strong, heavy our nets-the strain reached breaking point, and while 'twis dark we docked, and as we worked I felt as though new strength and steady joy surged through my being, so I sang a psalm, as David sang-a song to greet the morn; and then my heart was filled with quiet calm. The boat was soon in order, and we turned to dry and mend our nets. Then Jesus came-He called the boys, first John, then James, by name, and they arose and went and followed Him. I turned and gazed on Jesus standing there-He seemed to me all clothed in shining light as He stood in the pathway with the night behind Him and the dawn breaking around, His form so radiant and glad and free. And when He climbed the hill our sons went too-James was behind, and John was by

His side; and when they talked, John scarcely seemed our John-I felt that he had caught a marvellous light. And all my being seemed to overflow; I knew the night had passed-the dawn had come, and then I knew that we must let them go!" Letting go one of the attributes of expendability!

One of my favorite hymns in our hymnal is 'O Zion Haste' by Mary A. Thomson. Listen to these words and tell me if they don't sound like what Zebedee and Salome went through when they realized that their sons were expendable: "O Zion haste, they mission high fulfilling, to tell to all the world that God is light; that He who made all nations is not willing one should perish, lost in shades of night. Behold how many thousands still are lying, bound in the darksome prison house of sin, with none to tell them of the Saviour's dying, of the life He died for them to win. Proclaim to every people, tongue and nation, that God, in whom they live and move, is love: tell how He stooped to save His lost creation, and died on earth that man might live above. Give of thy sons to bear the message glorious; give of thy wealth to speed them on their way; pour out thy soul for them in prayer victorious; and all they spending Jesus will repay!"

I can honestly say I had such a father and mother in Wendell and Phyllis. I still remember the day that my father asked if I would stay on the family farm and take up the reins of responsibility as he did when he had gotten to my age. My dad was the fifth generation of Blackstones to farm the plot of land in the town of Perham since 1861. I would be the sixth from father to son to father to son six times over if I would, but I didn't. I felt I was being called elsewhere (the good news was my middle brother decided to follow the family tradition and Jay become number six) even then I didn't know where. My first thoughts was the army like my dad did then schooling to be a history teacher, but on the way down that path the Good Lord in 1970 called me like He did James and John. At the writing of this devotional 48 years have passed and my father passed into glory just a few weeks ago. My mother of 90 is still alive and I can say like the poem of Zebedee and Salome they had been nothing but supportive, if not proud! I had my father's funeral just a week ago and in my discourse I read a sermon dad preached many years ago called "the Road of Life'. In that sermon he mentioned his tour of duty for Uncle Sam in 1944-1946 and his return to take up the responsibility of being the next generation to farm the family homestead. He saw his calling, to plow the fields and milk the cows as a divine call just as he saw his son's calling into full-time Christian service. He sent his son and he supported his son to speed him on his way, and he always poured out his soul for that son. I will miss that prayer warrior, for I was expendable!

Will you silently watch as Christ calls your children into His service? It is now my turn as I have watched my boy go off to war, but cancer took him before he could fully follow God. My daughter on the other hand has been on the missionfield since 16 (a trip to Nigeria) and at 37 is serving the Lord in California. We are on opposite coasts, but I am so glad that my dad taught me the lesson of Zebedee: that kids are expendable!

9

ZACHARIAS—THE PRIVILEGED PRIEST

LUKE 1:20

And, behold, thou shalt be dumb, and not able to speak, until the day that these things shall be performed, because though believeth not my words, which shall be fulfilled in their season.

I BELIEVE THAT THERE IS for every Old Testament type a New Testament truth; a parallel, even in the area of people. If you don't believe that then I would have you compare the Old Testament Abram and Sara with the New Testament Zacharias and Elizabeth. Both reached old age without any hope of have a child and yet in both cases they did. Years ago I was reading this Our Daily Bread devotional and I loved the way Richard DeHaan from the Radio Bible Class described the story: "An angel of the Lord appeared to Zacharias as he was going about his duties in the Temple. Seeing this heavenly messenger, Zacharias was greatly troubled. 'But the angel said unto him, fear not, Zacharias: for thy prayer is heard; and thy wife Elizabeth shall bear a son, and thou shalt call his name John.' (Luke 1:13) This news seemed too good to be true, so Zacharias went on to ask for further proof. 'Whereby shall I know this?' (Luke 1:18) He inquired. The angel's word should have been sufficient, yet he wanted a sign. It was given him, but it involved something for which he had not bargained. The angel said, 'behold, thou shalt be dumb, and not able to speak . . . . .because thou believest not my words.' (Luke 1:20) And so Zacharias became speechless because of his unbelief! What a picture of many Christians today who are often silent because of the weakness of their faith." What do you think would be 'expendable' for unbelief?

So what do you think about questioning, or doubting the Lord? Some would say: "You should never question the Lord" while others would say: "you should only question God in faithfulness as you seek God's answer for something!" So what do you think? What do we know from the Bible? Abraham questioned the Lord (Genesis 18:23-33). Gideon questioned the Lord (Judges 6:36-40). Job and his friends questioned the Lord throughout their discourses (Job 2-32). David questioned the Lord often in his psalms (Psalm 4, 6, 10, 11, 15). You can find just about every saint in the Bible at one time or the other questioning the Lord. Mary after Zacharias would question Gabriel with: "How shall this be?" (Luke 1:34) Does a question always express doubt? No! Granted, doubt is wrong for any believer, and so is unbelief, but a sincere, honest question is not dishonoring to God. I have come to believe in my study that God loves for His child to seek an answer for a puzzling question that has come to light in their life. I feel that in the stories of Luke One we have the difference between the two: an honest question and a doubtful question.

Zacharias' question resulted in him being made speechless for nine months, whereas Mary's question brought no ill affects whatsoever, why? Because Zacharias' question was an unbelieving question: " . . . because thou believest not my words . . . " (Luke 1:20) You can't fool God. God not only knows your thought but the intend of your thoughts. Though sometimes the questions are similar but the heart is different. God can understand your question better than you can (John 2:24-25). If Zacharias had only remembered his Hebrew history and the story of Abram and Sara (Hebrews 11:11-12) and in faith believed; despite years of praying his was a doubtful heart (James 1:6-8). As for Mary there is no doubt in my mind that God heard a question of wonderment not doubt. When you think about it Mary's was a more difficult belief: a simple birth the normal way with Zacharias and Elizabeth or a birth without a husband? Reading the rest of the story we discover there was no rebuke of Mary by Gabriel, just a comforting explanation (Luke 1:35)! In the end Marry believed and accepted the angel's instruction, while Zacharias needed a sign which cost him his speech!

Someone has said: **"A man may be at his wit's end, but he need not be at his faith's end!"** Often we are perplexed by what God is doing in our lives; it is not wrong to quiz Him concerning the problem or the event, but questioning Him in doubt will only bring you more problems, just ask Zacharias. If you question honestly, longingly, and sincerely, you will find a loving, understanding answer in God's time. At the writing of this devotional our family is in such a time. Our 39-year old son suddenly came down with cancer just five months ago. He is across the street at the parsonage of the Emmanuel Baptist Church weakening every day. A once robust soldier-boy (United States Army) is now a shell of himself (60 pounds lost) and we wonder why? Like Zacharias I am not asking doubtfully, trustless, or faithlessly but in simple wonder. God's will is perfect even in cancer, and I will not question God foolishly (Job 1:22). I have known for a long time Paul's admonition to the young man Timothy: "But foolish and unlearned questions avoid, knowing that they do gender strifes." (II Timothy 2:23)

Despite Zacharias' doubt, he does teach us something about expendability. Anything is expendable in the mind of God when it comes to teaching His saint about trust; including one's sight, or one's walk, or one's speech. Zacharias was not the first or the last to be touched by God in the flesh. My mind goes back to the days of Jacob when he fought with God over his old nature. Remember, he was the deceiver, the trickster, the liar. But God had a purpose for Jacob, but before that purpose could be fulfilled he had to make Jacob into "Israel"! For most of his exile in Haran God worked on him. He made improvements, but by the time Jacob was heading back home there was still some work to be done. On the night of the fight on the banks of the Jabbok Stream, Jacob and the angel of God fought all night. Jacob wouldn't let go until he was changed, but there was price for that change, or maybe a reminder of that change; the angel touched Jacob's hip and the Scriptures simple end the encounter with these words: "And as he passed over Penuel the sun rose upon him, and he halted upon his thigh." (Genesis 32:32) Sometimes our struggles with doubt (remember, Jacob thought his brother was coming to slay him while God had promised at Bethel that he would protect him) ends with a handicap!

There are those who have always wondered what it was that caused Paul to call his infirmity a 'thorn in the flesh'? (II Corinthians 12:7) Once again there was something in Paul's body that was expendable to God. It never stopped Paul from finishing his mission, but it was a constant reminder that God's hand had been on his body. I have thought for years it had something to do with his conversion and his blindness (Acts 9), maybe, an eye problem for the rest of his life. Time would fail me to tell of Miriam

(Numbers 12) and others God touched physically. Remember, Jesus taught His followers that it would be better to go through life without an eye or a limb than to be eternally handicapped (Matthew 5:27–29). I believe that in knowing man's heart the Almighty knows what it will take for us to trust him. God knew that Zacharias had a big job ahead of him raising John the Baptist so nine months of silence were expendable in order to see through the years ahead without doubt. Read carefully the end of this story in Luke 1:57–77. In Zacharias' final statement we find a man full of faith because he knew what it was for God to strengthen his faith through His method of 'expendable'!

10

Isaac—The Sacrificial Son

Genesis 22:2

And He said, Take now thy son, thine only son Isaac, whom thou lovest, and get thee into the land of Moriah; and offer him there for a burnt offering upon one of the mountains which I will tell thee of.

CAN YOU IMAGINE BEING CALLED 'laughter'? Such was the meaning of the name of Abraham's and Sarah's son Isaac! Remember, Isaac was given that name to remind his aging parents that they had at first laughed at the angel's prediction that they would have a child in their old age. The good news is that faith (Hebrews 11:11-Romans 4:19-20) did take hold and Isaac, the child of promise, was born. So each time they called out Isaac's name they were reminded of this doubt. I have come to the belief this is also the reason for one of the greatest requests God ever made to man; to sacrifice that son, to see their son as expendable in the eyes of God. Do we have anything or anyone in our lives that reminds us of our faithlessness and God's faithfulness: **"If we believe not, yet He abideth faithful, He cannot deny Himself?"** (II Timothy 2:13) It is in events like this that we need to learn that what God gives He can take back. God is no 'Indian giver', but He does see His gifts to us as expendable in the molding of his man or woman. Is not this the lesson of Job as well (Job 1–2), and at the compiling of this chapter I too am experiencing this truth as the Good Lord in His wise providence is in the process of taking my 39-year old son home to glory through cancer!

Expendable

Isaac became 'the apple of his father's eye' after his miraculous birth. For all of his life Isaac was the gem of his mother's (Isaac was 37 at Sarah's death-Genesis 23:1) life and the pride of his father's (Isaac was 75 at Abraham's death-Genesis 27:7) life. Despite having their family late in life, both Abraham and Sarah were able to enjoy Isaac for many years, and that is what makes the sacrifice of Isaac such a trial of faith (Hebrews 11:17–19). Isaac was not only there 'only begotten son', but a son 'in whom they were well pleased'! Sound familiar? I believe we have before us the great trial of the Almighty Himself. When God sent forth His Son Jesus to the earth it was a trial greater than what Sarah and Abraham faced. Isaac was expendable to God, but was he expendable to Abraham? God the Father faced the same test in the redemption of mankind.

So often we read Genesis chapter 22 as only the trial of Abraham when in reality Sarah was on trial and so was Isaac himself. Sarah was no mentioned in the story, but you can't tell me she didn't know; mothers know these things especially when it deals with their sons. My wife Coleen is having a harder trial than I am. Don't get me wrong, I am suffering, but mothers suffer far worse than fathers when it comes to their children. When Isaac and Abraham left for Moriah the one that suffered worse was the one away. That person in our family trial is Scott's sister Marnie. Marine lives in California with her family of husband Josue and son Judah. Yesterday I put Marnie on a plane with her son for California. Marnie has made that cross-country trip eight times since her brother came down with lung cancer, a cancer that has spread throughout his body. But the one we often overlook in this trial is Isaac, for the one in the worst situation was Isaac, just like my son Scott. What you must see in this story is the 'Jehovah-Jireh' (Genesis 22:14), for the Lord God was also on trial in this story of Isaac and Abraham on Mount Moriah as I see the hand of the Good Lord in the situation with my dying son, a five and a half month struggle, as I write this 'expendable' story.

I like what F. B. Meyer writes in his devotional book "Great Verses Through the Bible" (Zondervan Publishing House 1966) on this trial of faith and I am convinced these line were written for me and my son and my family and I: "Abraham knew it would be. Probably, he never told Sarah (I don't agree) what God had asked of him till he and the lad were safely back in the tent. What need to trouble her? Her weak faith (I question this as well-Hebrews 11:11 and Romans 4:19–20) could not have stood the ordeal (my wife is proving that Sarah could have handled it). It was with an unfaltering tone that the patriarch told the young men that they two would presently return (Genesis 22: 5). Even though he should actually take Isaac's life, he was sure that he would receive him again from the altar in health. It was only at the very last moment that God indicated (Genesis 22:10) the ram as the sufficient substitute. So God's deliverances always come; they are provided in the mount of trial and sacrifice. When the foe seems secure of victory. So it was with Israel, Pharaoh, with his hosts, counted on an easy victory, the precipices around, the sea in front. To the eye of sense it seemed impossible to escape; all hope died! It was just then that the Almighty cleft a path through the mighty deep. (Exodus 14) 'In the fourth hour of the night.' Strength was well-nigh exhausted in the long battling with the waves. For hours the disciples with difficulty had kept themselves afloat. It seemed as if they must give in through physical collapse. It was then that the form of Jesus drew nigh unto the ship. (Matthew 14) On that night before execution. Thus Peter lies sleeping whilst the Church is gathered in prayer. Tomorrow he will be a corpse. But the angel comes then to open the prison doors. (Acts 12) So you many have come to an end of your own strength, and wisdom, and energy. The altar, the wood, and fire are ready, the knife is raised, your Isaac on the point to die; but even now God will provide. Trust Him to indicate the way of escape (I Corinthians 10:13)." How often Coleen and I have found that strength and energy and wisdom to deal with our son (165 days at this writing), and for those who think I only see a physical healing as God's provision; you are wrong! As I learned so many times with others a heavenly healing will be the best healing of all!

I have come to the belief in a study of 'expendable' things that God doesn't always ask us to sacrifice, but He does ask us to be willing to sacrifice. As with Abraham and many others after him, the Lord seems to give back what we thought He wanted. The widow of Nain's son comes to mind (Luke 7:11) and what about Lazarus (John 11:43); seemingly expendable, but in reality a test of this widow and the sisters. Only when we remember that all things, every person in our life can be used of God to try our faith (I Peter 1:6–7), just ask Job (Job 1:19). For me in my trial I recognize that God is using my son's sickness for some divine molding, shaping of my life and the lives of those around Scott. It is in this trial we will realize something about God and His purpose and plan that we would never understand or know without this ordeal. I might not know what it is yet, but I have discovered in tests of my past that without this testing something that needs to be done in the future will never happen; one is linked to the other by divine directive!

The greatest lesson I have learned from Abraham, Isaac, and Sarah, as I am learning from Scott, Coleen, and Marnie is the amazing parallels to what my God and His Son went through for me. Isaac was a beloved son so was Jesus (so is Scott). (Genesis 22:2-John 3:16). Isaac was a questioning son and so was Jesus. (So did Scott) (Genesis 22:7-Matthew 26:39). Isaac was a yielding son and so was Jesus. (So is Scott) (Genesis 22:9-Matthew 26:42) It took great faith by both parties to pass the test of Moriah, and so it was with the love of God and His willingness to give us His Son for our sacrifice; yes, Jesus was expendable. It is my prayer that we will come forth as gold in our trial of sacrifice!

11

Isaiah—The Pierced Prophet

Hebrews 11:37

.... sawn asunder ....

"I HAVE ALSO SPOKEN BY the prophets, and I have multiplies visions, and used similitudes by the ministry of the prophets." (Hosea 12:10) 'Similitude' simply means 'likeness.' In the context of Hosea's verse in which this word 'similitude' is used; it is speaking of the Lord using prophets not only to preach and prophecy His messages, but the prophets themselves were used by the Almighty as signs and wonders to teach the people of God, of God's ways. If you reread the Old Testament you will note how many times God uses 'similitudes' in relationship with His men. Remember the prophet that penned the verse on similitudes started his ministry by marrying a prostitute by God command to show the Israelites how that had prostituted themselves with idols (Hoses 1–3)! But for me, no Old Testament prophet was used more as a 'similitude' than the greatest of the prophets: Isaiah. If there was ever a man of God more expendable to God than Isaiah, I know not of one. If God can sacrifice an Isaiah on His altar of purpose and plan and providence than He can sacrifice anyone of us!

Isaiah had a long and distinguished career as a prophet of God. His name is found in the category of Elijah, Elisha, Samuel, Jeremiah, Ezekiel, and Daniel, as the best of the best. From the turbulent time of King Uzziah's death in 740 BC (Isaiah 6:1) to the terrible trial of Sennacherib's siege of Jerusalem in 701 BC, Isaiah was the constant voice of reason and understanding in a very difficult age for Judah. Almost from his first sermon God called Isaiah to speak out against the impending doom and gloom that would engulf the land unless Israel (northern kingdom) and Judah (southern kingdom) repent. One of the first 'similitudes' God uses in the life of Isaiah was at the naming of his firstborn son: Mahershalalhashbaz (yes, the longest name in the Bible). It was a name that meant that God's judgment on the nation was quickly coming (Isaiah 8:3–4). Isaiah was instructed to make a large banner and on that banner he was to write the meaning and put it up before the people like a neon billboard, so that each time an individual would pass the sign they could read the prophecy. (Isaiah 8:1–2) Each time Isaiah, or his wife, or any other person would speak the boy's name, it was a prophetic utterance. One of the things I have found expendable in God's doings is our families. As I write this article, we have had to bring in Hospice to help care for our son; he is dying of liver cancer! I have already lost another child, and when things like this happen there is no privacy in the life of a preacher or a prophet; all are fair game for God's work. As with Isaiah's family, God will use anyone and anything to get His message across.

For me, one of the strangest similitudes I found in Isaiah's life was the one in which the Good Lord commanded Isaiah: "Take off the sackcloth from your body, and the sandals from your feet, and he did so, going around stripped and barefoot. The Lord said, just as my servant Isaiah has gone stripped and barefoot for THREE YEARS, as a sign and protest against Egypt and Cush, so the king of Assyria will lead away stripped and barefoot the Egyptians captive and Cushite exiles, young and old, with buttock's bare, to Egypt's shame." (Isaiah 20:2–4 NIV) This was simply a dramatic similitude carried out by Isaiah for three years to prophesy the conquest of Egypt and Ethiopia (Cush) by the nation of Assyria. This wasn't even a Jewish prophecy, yet God humiliated and shamed his prophet by commanding him to live naked for three years to the public self-abasement that must have been the result. To persist for three years through, no doubt, the 'cat-calls', insults, laughter, pointings, and no doubt the call to put him away because he must have gone mad, crazy, insane! What we need to see before we get to the ultimate purpose of this chapter is that Isaiah's life, his complete life, everything in his life was inspired by God to deliver God's words to God's people. Sometimes Isaiah was the message; whether sermon or similitude, the meaning of either carried equal weight with God. For we also must be reminded that Isaiah didn't hid away in his home during those

Isaiah—the Pierced Prophet

three years, for I believe Isaiah walked around naked, exposing himself until the three years were up. Like with the big billboard, Isaiah was to be seen by the people and when they saw him stripped and barefoot they were told God's meaning. I have come to believe that sometimes our lives can say as much as our lips when it comes to delivering God's gospel. Are we willing to sacrifice our pride and privacy to show God to others?

The last lesson that I have for you from the amazing life of Isaiah comes more from Hebrew history than the Bible, but I have come to believe in Biblical events surrounding his death fall nicely into the doctrine of 'expendable', and I can't believe that Isaiah was not willing to lay down his life as a final similitude, a martyr's example. The ministry of Isaiah was certainly the tale of two Judah's. Isaiah was the leading and most outspoken prophet during the wonderful and wondrous days of revival and reform during the kingship of King Hezekiah. Recorded in II Kings and II Chronicles and his own book of Isaiah, these there the glory days of the latter kingdom age. However, these days were brought to an abrupt end when Hezekiah's son Manasseh took over. Those years (55 of them-II Kings 21:1) were some of the wickedest and evil days and Isaiah was there through some of them. Isaiah became a thorn in the side of wicked Manasseh. His evil deeds were legendary (II Kings 21:2-9), and it isn't surprising that he would come into direct conflict with God's mighty man of action and sermon.

According to the Jewish Talmud and the Palestinian Targum, Isaiah was caught up in Manasseh's purge (Just like James getting caught up in Herod's purge-Acts 12:1) and was murdered. II Kings 21:16 describes for us those days: "Moreover Manasseh shed innocent blood very much, till he filled Jerusalem from one end to another; besides his sin wherewith he made Judah to sin, in doing that which was evil in the sight of the Lord." Could there have been anyone more innocent than Isaiah? Sometimes we wonder why the wicked are allowed to prosper; why they are put in charge, and why they are allowed to kill the righteous. According to Hebrew tradition Isaiah was 'sawn asunder' with a wooden saw! There are many in the religious community that believe that is who Paul was referring to when he added those two words to his classic faith chapter; words I have printed above; words of expendability. In Paul's contrast to those that lived in glorious days of victory by 'faith' (Hebrews 11:33–35), but in mid-sentence Paul changes tone by speaking of the 'others' (Hebrews 11:35–38). I have come to believe that Isaiah died in the great Manasseh massacres. (Postscript: you must read II Chronicles 33:11–16 for the rest of the story of Manasseh; one of the greatest conversion stories of the Bible)

We are called on to "**. . . be faithful unto death . . .**" (Revelation 2:10) and I believe Isaiah was. As in life so in death Isaiah was a similitude to the people of God. Whether in the use of a son, or the symbol of a life, or in the end of days, we are to act in faith living and speaking the Word of God. Do we mirror the likeness of Christ (Romans 8:29) in our family, in our walk, and will we in our death? Ask yourself, who is watching my similitude for Christ? Am I willing to make my family, my walk, my life expendable?

12

James—The Disposable Disciple

Acts 12:1-2

Now about that time Herod the king stretched for his hands to vex certain of the Church. And he killed James the brother of John with a sword.

When Jesus called the brothers James and John to be His disciples, He gave them a surname: ***"the sons of thunder"!*** (Mark 3:17) I believe He did that to characterize their stormy disposition, tempestuous zeal, and fiery spirit. Later, if you remember, it was these same brothers who came to Jesus with the simple solution for dealing with the unbelieving Samaritan town that had rejected Christ's message: "And when His disciples James and John saw this they said, Lord wilt thou that we command fire to come down from heaven and consume them even as Elijah did?"(Luke 9:59) (The event they were referring to is found in II Kings 1:5-10!) Besides being prone to anger, they were also prone to ambition. Remember when they and their mother approached Jesus with a request to set on the right and the left of the throne in Jesus' Kingdom: "Grant unto us that we may sit one on thy right hand and the other on they left hand in they glory!" (Mark 10:37) Despite these shortcomings, James and John were trainable, teachable, and transformable and Jesus turned both of the lads of Zebedee into faithful apostles, and both were 'faithful unto death' (Revelation 2:10), but little did James know he would be the first and John the last to die; both expendable but in entirely different ways!

I find it interesting that Jesus should use these brothers to demonstrate the two extremes of discipleship: the long term discipleship of John and the short term discipleship of James. I would say that most Disciples of Christ would favorite the long-life discipleship of John even if that meant a tour of duty on Patmos (Revelation 1) verses the short-life expectancy of a martyr (Acts 12). Most historians believe that John lived through the bulk of the first century and maybe into the second; while James was one of the first to face a martyr's death, probably second to Stephen (Acts 7:60). James was certainly the first Apostle to give his life for the Cause of Christ, but he wasn't the last; their again early Church historian's record they all did except for perhaps John who died of old age in Ephesus? I can hear some saying all ready: 'What a Waste!' yet it appears that it was through the blood of Christ's expendable disciples that the Church expanded and eventually engulfed the Roman Empire: the famous 'blood of the martyrs'.

James typifies the old Roman coin with a picture on one side of an ox facing both an altar and a plow. On the other there is the inscription that reads: **"Ready for either!"** Some believers like Vance Havner (mid-80s) and G. Vernon McGee are called to a long life of service; while others like Nate Saint and Jim Elliot (martyrs in Ecuador in the 1950s in their 30s) are called on to share just a short life, a few days of service. I seem to be among the Vance and Vernon group as I near my 48th year in the pastorate. I have had the honor and privilege to preach over 50 years (1966–2020), and my health is good and I see many more days ahead by God's grace. But I am haunted by these words from Jim Elliot, quoted by his wife Elizabeth Elliot in her famous book "Through Gates of Splendor": "Am I ignitable? God deliver me from the dread asbestos of other things. Saturate me with the oil of the Spirit that I may be aflame. But Flame is transient, often short lived. Canst thou bear this my soul: short life? In me these dwell, the Spirit of the great short lived, whose zeal for God's house consumed Him. Make me thy fuel, Flame of God!" Such was the Spirit of Jesus (33) and James (probably also in his 30s). James, perhaps, more than any other mirrored the life and ministry of His Messiah. I am persuaded that after Pentecost James' ministry was even shorter than his Saviour's ministry of three years? James was disposable to the ministry, expendable to the Church.

One of my often referred to authors is Herbert Lockyer; he is best known for his "ALL" series of books about Biblical people, topics, and events. In his grand book of "All the Apostles of the Bible" (Zondervan Publishing 1959), he writes this on James' expendability:

James—the Disposable Disciple

"James was the first to feel the hostility of Herod, and the next to Stephen to win the honor of martyrdom in the early Church (Acts 12:1-4). Because the cruel death of James pleased the Jews, Herod then seized Peter and cast him into prison, and so the two conspicuous pillars of the Church became the victims of Herod's new found zeal for Jewry. Why James was honored by martyrdom under Herod, and Peter was spared from his cruelly, is one of the secrets of Him who moves in mysterious way His wonders to perform. After fourteen years (?) of strenuous witness, the best testimony of which was the jealously of Herod and the delight of the Jews over his death, there came James' obituary notice. The tyrant's sword ended a life laid on the altar, but James had no fear of those who could kill only the body. He was 'grit by the grace of God on every hand' and death could not separate the apostle from 'the love of God which is in Christ Jesus our Lord' (Romans 8:37-39). James was the apostolic protomartyr, the first of the number to gain the crown, cheerfully taking the cup which they had told their Lord they were ready to death. The Acts of the Apostles may not record one word James said, or any act he performed, but it does tell of his readiness to be offered as a sacrifice for Christ's sake. His ambitious daring distinguished his career but hastened his glory by glorious consummation. His noble rage and fiery zeal thrust him into the forefront of danger and brought him his baptism of blood in the cause of the truth which has ever defied the power of fire and sword . . . cultivating conscientious allegiance to God and to a Spirit-enlightened conscience, James rose above Herod and his sword bathed in blood to touch on bended knee the Royal Scepter of Heaven. Thus, he became greater in death than in life, for the sword of Herod was crossed by the Sword of the Spirit, and in the martyrdom of saints like Stephen and James, the immortal hope of the Gospel was liberated. 'Oh, my Thy soldiers, faithful, true, and bold, fight as the Saints who nobly fought of old, and win, with them, the victor's crown of gold, Alleluia.'"

I believe what happened after the death of Stephen (the scattering of the saints-Acts 8:1, 11:19) happened after the death of James resulting in no only the extension of the Church but its expansion! It has always resulted in the Church growing. A few years ago I got a personal and up close view of what happened when the world martyrs the saints. In Orissa (a state in India) the Church was scattered because of persecution, and yes, the death of a few saints. Instead of weakening the Church, it only strengthened the Church and instead of the Body of Christ being found in a few places in central Orissa the Church was so scattered that many other churches were started. I got to travel to these places in 2012 and see the results of what happens when James is killed. I still hear from this persecuted Church and still hear the rejoicing. In 2016, I returned to see a new church sanctuary that had just been built a living testimony that even the martyrdom of the Apostle can't stop the Church. The question remains, however, are we like James and Jim Elliot ready to a short-term ministry, a ministry that could ignite the next great expansion of the Church: it happened in Ecuador and it happened in Orissa just like in Jerusalem!

13

Lazarus—The Beloved Brother

John 12:1

Then Jesus six days before the Passover came to Bethany, where Lazarus was which had been dead, whom He raised from the dead.

Who of us has not heard of Lazarus of Bethany? With the exception of His own resurrection, many scholars believe that the resurrection of Lazarus was Christ's crowning miracle while here on earth. Let us consider in this chapter on the 'expendable', Lazarus' part in this extraordinary and exceptional historical event, and the reason God saw Lazarus as expendable; was this death for Lazarus' learning, or was it for Martha or perhaps Mary, or perhaps you, or me?

As we know Lazarus' sickness (John 11:1) was a sickness unto death. As I write this article my 39-year old son has just died. His was a lung and liver cancer that was a sickness unto death (it only took six months for the cancer to consume his body). Being in the ministry for 44 years now, I have visited many people in the hospital who were supposed to recover, but died. I have also visited many in the hospital that were supposed to died, but lived! That is why the message of Isaiah to King Hezekiah is important for everyone to consider: "In those days was Hezekiah sick unto death . . . Thus saith the Lord. Set thine house in order for thou shalt die and not live!" (II Kings 20:1) As with Hezekiah, so with my son Scott, the shock of a terminal illness was shocking. Unlike Hezekiah and Lazarus, Scott did die, but not before setting his house in order.

By God's grace Hezekiah like Lazarus lived a number of years longer; for Hezekiah it was 15 years (II Kings 20:6), but for Lazarus the number is not given. The challenge for us is that each of us needs to always have our house in order, for we never know when the Good Lord will call; just remember the rich farmer's story (Luke 12:16–21)! One of the very earliest saying I claimed for my life was this simple but profound sentence: **"A Christian lives in such a way that he is always ready to die!"** Are you? Are you ready to die so that someone else might be ready to live? In the tragedy of my soldier-son, we have seen his sudden departure affect others still living, and sometimes that is the only purpose we can find in the death of someone so young. Sometimes when we look at the face in the coffin we should realize that it was for us they died, not for them!

I have heard so many people say at the death of a loved one, if God loved them why did He let them die? We know that Jesus loved Lazarus (John 11:3, 5), yet he died. Even while Lazarus was dead the people acknowledged that Jesus loved Lazarus (John 11:36). Just because you get sick and might even die from that sickness, it doesn't mean that God doesn't love you. Paul would write these classic lines in Romans: "For I am persuaded that neither death . . . . ..shall be able to separate us from the love of God which is in Christ Jesus our Lord." (Romans 8:38–39) It is interesting to me that the first subject that Paul mentions is death. It is because death is the most feared event in our lives, but still our greatest encouragement in life or death is that Jesus still loves us (I John 4:10). Recently I found this line from a Gospel song sung by a group called "Legacy Five" that says: "No matter what happens tomorrow, Jesus will love us still!"

So if Jesus loved Lazarus why did He tarry? (John 11:6) Why did Jesus let Lazarus die when He had the power to keep him alive? (John 11:37) Jesus gave the answer before he resurrected Lazarus from the grave: "This sickness is not unto death, but for the glory of God that the Son of God might be glorified thereby." (John 11:4) Lazarus; death was not as some teach: the chastisement of God, or the judgment of God. Lazarus was not ill through some sin. Lazarus was like the man born blind, an instrument to magnify and glorify the works of God (John 9:3). F. B. Meyer once wrote in "Great Verses Through the Bible": **"The child of God is often called on to suffer (and may I add die) because there is nothing that will convince onlookers of the reality and power of true religion as suffering will do!"**

Lazarus—the Beloved Brother

The end result of Jesus use of Lazarus was: "Then many of the Jews which came to Mary, and had seen the thing which Jesus did believed on Him." (John 11:45) Later Lazarus was in danger for John also writes: " . . . the chief priests consulted that they might put Lazarus also to death, because that by reason of him many of the Jews went away and believed on Jesus." (John 12:10-11) How many lives have been gloriously changed because somebody got a terminal illness, or died in a tragic way? How many individuals have gotten saved because of the death of a loved one? Expendable for an eternal good is a practice of the Almighty. Whenever I preach on the Lazarus resurrection I always make mention of the fact that in looking for a miracle you can find one in any healing, but the greater miracle is in a resurrection! (Something ahead for my son!)

Once again I turn to the pen of F. B. Meyer (Great Verses Through the Bible) to finish our thoughts on the expendability of Lazarus, for Meyer's believed as I do that Lazarus' death was for another: "Yes, we shall see the glory of God. (John 11:40) We shall see the graves give up their dead, not only at the last day but now. Thousands around us are dead in trespasses and sins (Ephesians 2:1), in which they walk according to the course of this world. Alas! More than this, they stink in the putridity of their lives and speech. Around their graves gather their friends and relatives, bathed in tears, but unable to arrest the progress of decay. But, if we will believe, we shall see the glory of God. But how shall we believe for this? It seems easy to some to believe. The Marys, who sit at the Lord's feet, feeding on His words, find the life and the light of faith in His beloved presence. But others, like Martha, are distracted with so many things, that faith seems impossible. And this is the very point where this story is so abundantly helpful. Jesus must have the cooperation and sympathy of someone's faith before this miracle could be wrought-and these He found, not in Mary, as we might have expected, but in Martha, the harassed housewife. In educating Martha in this stupendous act of faith: 1) the Lord gave her a distinct promise-'Thy brother shall rise again'; 2) He drew her attention from His words to Himself, who lay beneath and behind them: 'I am the resurrection and the life'; 3) He forced her to confess her faith. To express it would confirm and increase it: 'Believeth thou this?' 4) He compelled her to act on the faith He had created, by allowing the bystanders to remove the stone. All her soul woke up as she remarked these preparations for her brother's resurrection. She believed; and her faith gave the Lord the pivot on which His leverage might rest!"

So which do you believe about death and dying? Is it for the dying one, or the living ones? Was it for Lazarus or his sisters Mary and Martha, or maybe the mourners? As I write and think of my son's homegoing just five days ago, I am still looking for who this was for. I know I learned a lot of lessons, teaching of God that I wouldn't have seen or experienced any other way, but what of my wife, our church family, Scott's sister and family, and yes, that stranger that was watching to see how we would reacts to this the most serious of all trials. I am constantly reminded of Paul's admonition in I Corinthians 10:31: "Whether therefore ye eat or drink (or watch a son die) or whatsoever you do (care for a son to his final breath), do all to the glory of God." This must be the final action even when God thinks our loved ones are expendable to His ultimate glory!

14

Samson—The Strongman Slave

Judges 16:30

And Samson said, let me die with the Philistines. And he bowed himself with all his might; and the house fell upon the lords, and upon all the people that were therein. So the dead which he slew at his death were more than they which he slew in his life.

Samson came into this world as few do. Like Isaac his conception in a barren womb was unique. Like Jacob his parents knew what he would become before he was born. Like Moses he was selected to deliver his people from oppression. Like Samuel he was presented to the Lord at an early age because of his special mission. Like John the Baptist his birth was predicted by an angel's visit. Like Jesus he was given tremendous abilities unmatched by any human before him or after him. Perhaps, few in human history had such expectations because of his coming, yet despite these wonderful privileges, honors, and endowments, Samson was one of the greatest disappointments of all times. Samson would be expendable, but not as most expected. If Samson would have died on a battlefield fighting the Lord's battles, we might have seen value in his life. If Samson would have died in old age having faithfully fulfilled the mission he had been born for, then we might have seen a glory in his death. But Samson didn't die in battle or in his bed, but in a pagan temple in a foreign land being made sport of by his enemies and the foes of his people. Willy Mullen once said: **"The best** *__of men are men at best!__* and Samson was one of those men, and when sin ruins a life then that life is expendable!

Samson's accomplishments were spectacular and downright amazing resulting in his being numbered in the Hall of the Famous Faithful recorded in Hebrews Eleven by the pen of the Apostle Paul: "And what shall I more say? For time would fail me to tell of . . . Samson . . . who stopped the mouth of lions . . . escaped the edge of the sword . . . out of weakness was made strong, valiant in fight, turned to flight the armies of the aliens." (Hebrews 11:32–34) His singlehanded victories over the lion (Judges 14:5–6), the thirty Philistines (Judges 14:19), catching three hundred foxes (Judges 15:4), and killing a thousand warriors with a jawbone of an ass (Judges 15:15) rank him as one of the top fighters of all time, and an elite Biblical warrior. The mention that in four separate occasions ' . . . the Spirit of the Lord came mightily upon him . . . ' (Judges 13:15, 14:6, 14:19, and 15:14) is the most I could find of any Old Testament saint! Add to that his feat of carrying the city gates of Gaza over twenty miles to Hebron (Judges 16:1–3) and Samson does go down in history as an Atlas, the strongest man in the world, a real human Hercules, yet from his first visit to a Philistine town a spiritual cancer began to grow in Samson's soul that was going to make him in twenty years expendable (Judges 16:31).

Despite all of Samson's tremendous victories and marvellous feats, God's strongman was a miserable failure. Samson's fall from grace is recorded in Judges sixteen and chronicles the sad downfall and decline of a man of faith. It didn't happen suddenly, overnight, in a day or in one event. It was, as all falls are, a gradually spiral as 'the lust of the flesh' (I John 2:15) got hold of every part of Samson's being. From day one Samson had ' . . . a sin that so easily beset . . . ' him (Hebrews 12:1). Samson's sin: 'strange women' (Proverbs 5:3–23, 7:5–27). Samson's weakness for Philistine women was stronger than his superhuman strength. Three times in the Judges' account it speaks of his unlawful relationship with these 'strange women' (Judges 14:1, 16:1, and 6:4); the last one, Delilah would take his life. The saddest commentary on this whole sad, sorted, affair is that Samson knew " . . . not that the Lord was departed from him." (Judges 16:20). By now you know one of my favorite devotional writes is the Englishman F. B. Meyer and his great book on "Great Verses Through the Bible". I like what he wrote about Samson and the warning Samson's life proclaims: "Beware of unconscious deterioration! Grey hairs may be there and there upon us without our knowing it. The Lord may be gone out on feet so noiseless, that

Samson—the Strongman Slave

we are not aware that His Spirit has glided along the corridor, and through the doorway, whispering, 'Let us depart'. Deterioration is unconscious because it is gradual. The rot that sets in on autumn fruit is very gradual. The damp that silences the violin or piano does it work almost imperceptibly. Satan is too knowing too plunge us into some outrageous sin at a bound. He has sappers and miners engaged long before the explosion, in hollowing subterranean passages through the soul, and filling them with explosives. Spiritual declension blunts our sensibility. The first act of the burglar is to gag the voice that might alarm, and poison the watch-dog. So, sin blinds our eyes, and dulls our keen alertness to the presence of evil. Thus, the stages of our relapse are obvious to all eyes but our own. We are drugged as we are being carried off captives. The progress of evil within us is a matter of unconsciousness, largely because we are quick to discover reasons to justify our decadence. We gloze over the real state of affairs. We call sins by other names. We insist on considerations which in our eyes appear to justify our conduct. We still attend to our religious duties, and try to persuade ourselves that it is with us as in time past." Is not that an expert look into what happened to the judge Samson; the strongman who became a slave to 'strange women'?

Samson's hair was only the outward sign of his power, for he had long since lost his inward strength in the Lord, long before his haircut. I have come to believe that Samson was just an ordinary human, like anyone of us, but what made him special and strong was 'the Spirit of the Lord'. His strength came from the Lord and the Lord alone and for a time Samson would rest on his past exploits, his reputation if you will. But Meyer's was right when he coined the phrase 'unconscious deterioration' for that is exactly what happened as year after year passed and Samson spent more time flirting with 'strange women' than communicating with the Lord! So what is the result of being a careless judge, or let us make it personal: a careless Christian?

A few years ago in a study of the life of Samson I came up with this list: 1) BLINDNESS-unaware at first just what is happening (Judges 16:21); just like the story of David and Bathsheba (II Samuel 11); 2) BONDAGE-brought under the control of Satan, sinners, or a sin (Judges 16:21), to work at their mill without pay or pride; 3) BELITTLED-by the enemies of God and God's people (Judges 16:23), exhibited as a trophy of their power and put on display as a failure; and 4) BURIED-with them with a dead testimony (Judges 16:30), your usefulness over, a castaway (I Corinthians 9:27).

Samson had feet of clay, and an Achilles' heel. Satan knows our every weakness and he will exploit it to his advantage and our disadvantage. Unless we keep the shield of faith (Ephesians 6:16) up, constantly, and never let it down for a moment it is our only hope. When Samson saw a pretty Philistine he put his shield down, he dropped his guard, and he lost his head. His parents tried to warn him (Judges 14:3), and even God knew that Samson would fail. I remember the first time I really saw these words in the angel's first statement to Samson's mother: " . . . and he SHALL BEGIN to deliver Israel out of the hands of the Philistines." (Judges 13:5) God knew Samson couldn't finish the job!

15

Joseph—The Stunned Stepfather

Matthew 1:19

Then Joseph her husband, being a just man, and not willing to make her a publick example, was minded to put her away privily.

Joseph was the foster-father of Jesus. Joseph was the husband of Mary, the mother of our Saviour. Joseph was the son of Jacob, a New Testament truth from another Old Testament type, a descendant of the original Jacob and Joseph (Matthew 1:2). Joseph was the stepfather of the Christ. I have always believed that Joseph has been ignored in the telling of the Christmas story; the innkeeper (Luke 2:7) seems to get more lines in the Christmas play and we don't even know his name and if you look carefully at the Scriptures he isn't even mentioned! I could add the unnamed wise men (Matthew 2) and the unnamed shepherds (Luke 2) and their parts in the greatest story ever told, and yet in the nativity scenes they are out front while Joseph is tucked away in the shadows in a corner of the make-believe stable (which was probably a cave not a wooden structure)! Sometimes it seems that the animals of the Christmas story get more press than Joseph and we aren't even sure there was a donkey, or 'oxen feeding on hay'! Admittedly, there does seem to be more colorful parts in this divine play than Joseph's with the angels suddenly appearing to the shepherds 'while they watch their flocks by night', or the marvel of the 'Star' that lead the wise men from afar, but we should never forget the vital role Joseph would play both before Christmas and after Christmas. Joseph's part was the 'expendable' part of the Christmas story. Joseph's fatherhood was expendable to the doctrine (Galatians 4:4) of Christ's coming; Joseph's rights as husband were expendable to the Christmas theology: "And knew her not till she had brought forth her firstborn son: and he called His name Jesus." (Matthew 1:25) Joseph would eventually be willing to give up all his rights, honors, and privileges of a man, a husband, and a father (remember, Joseph would eventually be a father to four sons and at least two daughters-Mark 6:3) to care for the Son of God. This is why I add Joseph to our list of 'expendables'!

Joseph was distinguishable in his BEGAT (Matthew 1:1–17). In reality, the genealogy of Matthew One is the human genealogy of Joseph not Jesus because Jesus never came through the bloodline of Joseph. You will find the human genealogy of Jesus recorded in Luke 3:23–38 where His human line is traced back to God; whereas Joseph's line simply goes back to Abraham. Note carefully: "Joseph, the husband of Mary, of who was born Jesus." (Matthew 1:16) Joseph had no part in the conception of Jesus (Luke 1:35 and Matthew 1:25). Despite this, Joseph was not chosen by chance or circumstance, for it was important that the bloodline of faith (Matthew 1:2) flow through his reins as well; much more the royal line of David (Matthew 1:6). When the angel (I believe Gabriel) greeted Joseph for the first time to tell him what was happening to his beloved Mary, Joseph was addressed as " . . . thou son of David . . . " (Matthew 1:20) Remember of all the men of Judah Joseph was chosen, just like of all the virgins of Judah Mary was chosen. Granted, Joseph would play a secondary role, a shadow role, a supportive role, but his was a vital role and in that role Joseph was willing to give up his business, his hometown, his nation, and his homeland for a while just to protect a baby that wasn't even his own; that's expendable!

Joseph was distinguishable in his BETROTHAL (Matthew 1:18). The Old King James calls this an 'espousal'. This arrangement lasted for at least a year, and during that time it was binding as a marriage except the couple stayed with their own families. The only way the espousal could be broken was through a divorce. When the news of Mary's pregnancy was learned Joseph was stunned, but took the righteous course, the kind course in seeking a divorce, but quietly (Matthew 1:19). Joseph had every right to bring Mary before the courts and see that she was condemned for this unjustifiable transgression. Joseph tells us a lot about his character by taking the compassionate course; that is until the angel showed up. I see the deep love of Joseph for Mary in this attitude which for me brings to light another

Joseph—the Stunned Stepfather

aspect of Joseph's expendability and that being the loss of his reputation! What would people think of Joseph when they learned that Mary was carrying somebody else's child, even if as they said it was God's Child? I feel that one of the reasons Joseph was chosen is the fact that he carried with him the same characteristic of his adopted son: "But made himself of no reputation, and took upon him the form of a servant . . . " (Philippians 2:7) As far as Joseph was concerned his reputation was expendable to the ultimate purpose and divine plan of the Almighty.

Joseph was distinguishable in his BETHLEHEM (Luke 2:1–20). Remember, Joseph was also of the house and lineage of David (Luke 2:4) which made Bethlehem Joseph's ancestral hometown. Joseph served the Lord in caring for the mother of the Christ in her labor (who else delivered the baby-I know of this feeling for I helped deliver my son Scott); the young baby after the birth, for who else found even the stable? Then it was off to Jerusalem (five miles away) on the eighth day (Luke 2:21) to see that Jesus fulfilled the Levitical law! Then it was back to Bethlehem to wait the wise men (Matthew 2:11). Warned by the same angel to flee the land, Joseph took his family out of harm's way, and I believe living on the gifts of the wise men stayed in Egypt until the angel told him it was safe. Joseph life was now expendable to the leading of the Lord and he proved himself faithful in each move, every instruction!

Joseph was distinguishable in Jesus' BOYHOOD (Luke 2:21–52). After the years in Egypt, Joseph brought his family back to the only life he knew and to the only town he knew and to a place where the Christ-Child could grow up with few dangers. I feel Joseph was a typical Jewish father; first, instructing his stepson in a trade: carpentry (Mark 6:3) which could mean in wood, but it could also mean in stone; Jesus could have been a mason! Joseph took Jesus annually to Jerusalem (Luke 2:41). Unlike Samuel, Jesus was not left at the Temple to be brought up by the priests, but throughout Jesus' boyhood Joseph was the man of his life. This tells me a lot of the character and quality of the man Joseph. The Eternal Father, when He was looking for an earthly father to care for His son He chose Joseph, for me, there is no greater recommendation than that. Whatever you might think of Joseph and his part in Christ's story part of the reason that " . . . Jesus increased in wisdom and stature and in favour with God and man . . . " (Luke 2:52) was the man Joseph. The boyhood of Jesus is described this way in Luke's Gospel: "And the child grew, and waxed strong in spirit, filled with wisdom; and the grace of God was upon Him." (Luke 2:40) Some of the credit for this development must be given to Joseph! Because Joseph leaves the Biblical scene somewhere in the boyhood of Jesus we don't know of the ultimate effect of this man on Jesus life. Some say Joseph was much older than Mary and died early, for that I know not, but this I believe. Joseph, like John the Baptist, knew that he would decrease and Jesus would increase (John 3:30)!

For most of us, Joseph is more like the part we play in people's lives. Ours is not the leading role, or even the secondary role. We simply pop in and out helping where we can; willing to sacrifice all, expend all that others might fulfill their God's determined destiny.

16

Philemon—The Beloved Brethren

Philemon 18

If he hath wronged thee, or oweth thee ought, put that on mine account.

Though there is no evidence that Paul ever evangelized the cities of the Lycus Valley in the ancient district of Asia Minor (modern day Turkey), it is clear that the man Philemon was brought to the faith by Paul himself! (Philemon 19) It is my opinion that Philemon probably meet Paul in Ephesus (Acts 19:10); was converted and took the Gospel back to the Phrygian city of Colosse. Both the Book of Philemon and the Book of Colossians were written and delivered at the same time (Colossians 4:7–15). This is certainly speculation on my part, but I believe the simple story of Philemon and Onesimus is another 'expendable' teaching found in God's inspired Word!

Because we know little about Philemon, it begs the question of why we would use him as another illustration in this series of devotionals on the doctrine of Biblical 'expendability'. If I have learned anything in this study it is that God doesn't ask everybody to sacrifice the same thing. If you will remember each of our fifteen expendables to this point have been different; granted, there have been a few similarities but the individual and the situations have been different; just like with Philemon. What might be found on God's list of expendable things will probably be assuredly not on your list! What we have been trying to do is to read carefully and examine carefully the text and the context of each story to discover exactly what God has asked the individual to give up, and so we follow the same pattern with Philemon. We must be willing to ask this question of ourselves as we go through life to know what the Lord wants on 'the altar of sacrifice'? Just recently, my family was asked to lay our 39-year old son on that altar!

Philemon, in my opinion, was the recipient of Paul's most personal letter. Timothy and Titus got some personal letters, but not as specific as Philemon's. It is a touching epistle of brotherly love and forgiveness. It seems as if one of Philemon's slaves, Onesimus, had stolen (Philemon 11) something from his master, and then ran off to hide from the law of the slave and the master. For a while Onesimus was able to elude escape, but eventually he was caught by the authorities and was thrown in a prison, and guess that his cellmate became? I have come to believe that Paul and Onesimus meet in Rome while Paul was waiting his court date with Caesar (Acts 28:30–31), or in perhaps another cell, for we should never forget that when Paul came into a new town he checked out the jail before the motel because the odds were that Paul would be thrown in prison first. It was during their time in prison together that Onesimus was converted by Paul (Philemon 10). Eventually, Onesimus was released from jail and sent back home with Paul desiring the same for himself (Philemon 22). With the prodigal went a letter of explanation and exhortation. That epistle would one day get into the New Testament Canon as the Epistle of Paul to Philemon, one of five one chapter books of the Bible, but also one of the most powerful! For me the book is summed up in the four words of Philemon 9: " . . . yet for love's sake . . . " Love is always a factor in expendability. Unless there is a love of God there will be no willingness to 'give up what you cannot gain to gain what you cannot lose.' Read carefully Matthew 16:24–26 before you read on!

From that letter we learn that Philemon was a well-to-do member of the Christian community of Colosse. At least one of the local churches of that large town met in Philemon's house (Philemon 2). Paul was on first name terms with his wife Apphia and their son Archippus. In the eyes of Paul he was a beloved brother, a fellow worker in the Cause of Christ. I have always loved the concept of the 'house church' and Philemon seemed well established in the community and the Church. Rare today is the family that opens their home to such a ministry in the Body of Christ. I am convinced that the teachers of the Bible explained quite clearly that whatever we have in the way of possessions are really not our own; they belong to Jesus; your cars, homes, boats, camps by the shore, things and all that stuff in the storage locker! There are a lot of these things God could and would use if we made them available to Him. Even like Philemon we need to allow God to us the people of our lives. We might not have any slaves but maybe we have employees. I have a deacon who owns a construction company and over the forty-seven years I have been the pastor of the Emmanuel Baptist Church Greg has done a lot of construction on church property. More often than not he does the work for nothing, but he still has to pay the men who work for him, but for that day they are serving the Lord. I believe all that we have must be dedicated to the Great Commission; all is expendability, even a servant! Someone has said, **"Every Christian should determine that wherever he has a home, God should have an altar!"** I will simply add on that altar everything in our lives, things and people need to be sacrificed!

I know that Onesimus must have had misgivings as he worked his way back home. No doubt he had questions about Paul's instructions and what his master Philemon would do or say. Yet the indication from Church historians suggests that when Onesimus returned that Philemon did exactly what Paul suggests. An unknown poet wrote this: "Happy the home when God is there, and love fills every breast. When one their wish, and one their prayer, and one their healthy rest. Lord let us in our hearts agree, thy blessed home to gain. Unite our hearts in love of Thee, and love to all will reign." When Onesimus got home I believe he found like the prodigal in Jesus famous parable (Luke 15:11–32) forgiveness and love waiting at the door, or like the prodigal son did Philemon meet Onesimus down the path? I believe Philemon was one of those followers of Christ that was willing to give all (Luke 14:33), so dealing with a runaway slave wasn't really an issue, for once all is on the altar of sacrifice the simple changes that happen beyond your control will not affect your expendability.

Church tradition tells us that eventually Philemon became the Bishop of Colosse and with his dear wife and beloved son and faithful servant Onesimus lost his life during the terrible purge and persecution of the infamous Nero. Whether or not this is true is hard to verify, but in my opinion this would be a logical and spiritual end to a man like Philemon, for many of the early Church were "... faithful unto death ..." (Revelation 2:10). Their homes were expendable; their things were expendable; their families were expendable; their slaves were expendable, and their lives were expendable because once one thing becomes that way other things are asked: expendable-too faithful to live very long! Are you willing to forgive a brother a hurt, an offense, or a loss? What about an employee that steals from you? A son that disrespects you? Are you willing to forgive and forget even to your own hurt financially? Are you willing to lose property to forgive? Forgiveness more often than not requires some kind of loss; expendable!

Philemon is a good example of this series because he was a member of a group of early Christians that were willing to put their lives, their lifestyles, and their love on the altar of expendability. This is our last point and that being that expendability must be 'willingly', not necessity as Paul taught us in his letter to Philemon! (Philemon 13–14)

17

ENOCH—THE TRANSLATED TYPE

HEBREWS 11:5

By faith Enoch was translated that he should not see death; and was not found, because God had translated him: for before his translation he had this testimony, that he pleased God.

THE BIBLE TELLS US THE history of Enoch in a few short verses: "And Enoch walked with God after he begat Methuselah three hundred years, and begat sons and daughters; and all the days of Enoch were three hundred and sixty-five years: and Enoch walked with God: and he was not; for God took him." (Genesis 5:22–24) The other verse on Enoch printed above tells us this walking relationship pleased God and that was the reason Enoch was translated. So what was it about this walk with God that so impressed God that he would change the natural order (' . . . it is appointed upon man once to die . . . ' Hebrews 9:27) and make Enoch an exception to the rule of death? Note, in the Genesis 5, the obituary chapter of the Bible, that they all died a physical death but Enoch. We must know what it was about Enoch that changed God's mind lest we miss the next major translation recorded in the Scripture and that being the rapture of the Church (I Thessalonians 4:16–17). So what was it about Enoch's life that put Enoch in God's list of expendable; to take him out of the world long before his relatives and his contemporaries? The Bible reveals that only one other man never saw death as all others before or after Enoch experienced; and that was the great

Hebrew prophet Elijah (II Kings 2:11–18); both were expendable, and now we know that this doctrine applies to both the living and the dead. A man by the name of Howard Arnold Walters in 1907 wrote these lines for a Church hymn under the title of "I Would Be True": "I would be true, for there are those who trust me; I would be pure for there are those who care. I would be strong, for there is much to suffer; I would be brave, for there is much to dare." Enoch was such a man and this is why I believed he was translated!

First, Enoch is called the seventh from Adam (Jude 14, I Chronicles 1:30). Seven is the number of perfection in the Bible, but the significance is not seven for there are a lot of unrighteous sevens in the Bible, but the seventh from Adam. That makes Enoch a part of the godly line (Genesis 4:26). It is my opinion that is way the man Enoch pleased God. Those who keep the faith are well pleasing to God: "But without faith it is impossible to please him: for him that cometh to God must believe that he is, and that he is a rewarder of them that diligently seek him." (Hebrews 11:6) This is the key ingredient both in the days of Enoch and in our days. Jesus wondered: "Nevertheless when the Son of Man cometh, shall He find faith on the earth?" (Luke 18:8) There are a lot of things that are expendable in this world and in our relationship with God, but faith isn't one of them.

Second, Enoch not only was a part of the godly line; he was also a part of the Messianic line (Luke 3:37). We often overlook that the Matthew genealogy was through Jesus' adopted father Joseph (Matthew 1:1–18), but Jesus' divine line went through Mary back to God. So Enoch was also of the royal line (David), so this combination of godly, royal, and Messianic would be well-pleasing to God. The Holy Writ is clear; unless we can trace our spiritual line back to Christ we will not be pleasing to God.

Third, Enoch was also listed in the faithful line (Hebrews 11:5). So what was the faith of Enoch? I mentioned at the beginning of this chapter of Enoch's walking kind of faith, but what was it after 65 years that set Enoch's feet walking with God. Genesis 5:21–22 seems to give us only one answer: the birth of Enoch's son Methuselah, but what would the birth of a boy have such a changing effect on Enoch's life? The answer is in the meaning of Methuselah's name: "when he dies it shall come"! It was in that meaning for the next 300 years Enoch walked with God and gave us a timeless principle: "Faith cometh by hearing and hearing by the Word of God." (Romans 10:17) And that too would be well pleasing to God. Someone has written: **"When faithfulness is most difficult, it is most necessary!"** I have come to believe the prophecy Enoch was told about through the birth of his son was the coming flood judgment on the world. If you trace the ages of the men of Genesis 5 you will discover the year of the Noah Flood was the same year of Methuselah's death; 969 years after Enoch named his son Methuselah!

Lastly, Enoch was also of the prophet's line (Jude 14). There are some Scriptural scholars that believe Enoch was the first of the prophets that can be traced in the Bible, but the prophecy he is most famous for Biblically is not Noah's Flood, but the Lord's return with ten thousands of His saints (Jude 14)! The flood prophecy has been fulfilled but the coming of Christ is still on the books. So a man that is still proclaiming the coming of Christ is a man that is well-pleasing to God. One of the reasons the Lord left His disciples behind was to foretell His return (Acts 1:8, 11). Paul's first epistle was probably I Thessalonians and the theme of that letter is the return of Christ, even the prediction of the rapture, the translation of the Church. But will He find the faith of an Enoch still on the earth. During Enoch's time the faithful where very few as they are today compared to the earth's population. I love these words from the pen of Richard DeHaan of the Radio Bible Class and their classic daily devotional, Our Daily Bread article in the 1960s: "One of the most heroic stories to come out of the Korean War involved a young sergeant by the name of Gardolibov. He had been engaged in the severe fighting on Heartbreak Hill. When the shooting had subsided, a rescue team was dispatched to the area to aid the wounded. The sergeant was found dying, but they discovered something very unusual. Although his hands were paralyzed, he had clinched between his teeth the two ends of a communication wire that had been broken. In that moment when one would expect his every thought and concern to be directed towards his own needs, he was still doing what he could to keep the messages going through. He was faithful unto death! Many so-called 'soldiers-of-the-cross' are put to shame by this noble example. Sad to say, when the going gets rough, the demands get great, the sacrifice too costly, or the shame of the cross too much to bear; they desert their post and flee to the back lines where it's more comfortable and secure. Some even go AWOL. O what might be accomplished in our warfare against the powers of evil if only we had more in our ranks like Sergeant Gardolibov: men and women, boys and girls, who are sold out to the cause of Christ that they remain true to their calling? Regardless of the circumstances, they do everything in their power to make sure the 'message' goes through. If it were up to you, would the Good News of the Gospel be communicated? In the battle against sin, let us recognize our responsibility to the Captain of our salvation (Hebrews 2:10), and be so dedicated to His cause that whether 'by life or death', Christ will be magnified."

What kind of testimony do you have? Who are you seeking to please? Paul wrote to the churches of Galatia: "For do I now persuade men or God? Or do I seek to please men? For if I yet please men I should not be the servant of Christ." (Galatians 1:10) We live just as much in the days of Enoch as in the days of Noah (Matthew 24:37). Are you ready to be translated? Translation seemly means "a change of position". Rapture is not a Biblical term, just a theological one, so let us live pleasing to God that we are translated!

18

Ishmael—The Troubled Teenager

Genesis 16:11–12

And the angel of the Lord said unto her, Behold, thou art with child, and shalt bear a son, and shalt call his name Ishmael; because the Lord hath heard thy affliction. And he shall be a wild man; his hand will be against every man, and every man's against him; and he shall dwell in the presence of all his brethren.

Ishmael was one of those rare individuals in Scripture whose parents were told beforehand of his birth and what kind of person he would be when he grew up. What they were not told was their firstborn son would be expendable in God's overall plan for their family's history and the world's history. Recently, I was rereading Paul's great last epistle, both to Timothy, and his last overall I believe. It was as I pondered the life of Ishmael I began to understand what Paul meant when he wrote: "But in a great house (Abraham's home) there are not only vessels of gold (Isaac) and silver (Ishmael), but also of wood (Isaac) and of earth (Ishmael); and some to honor (Isaac), and some to dishonor (Ishmael)." (II Timothy 2:20) I have come to believe that this one New Testament verse speaks volumes of the Old Testament house of Abram and his two sons and the two mothers of that home!

Ishmael was the first son of Abraham, but certainly not the last; we know of Isaac but what of the sons from his third wife Keturah? (Genesis 25:1–4) Ishmael was born to Sarah's handmaid Hagar. This birth came about because of the impatience of Sarah and Abraham and the long delayed arrived of their promised son Isaac. They decided to help God out a bit by invoking a local tradition and that of the Mistress's maiden being a surrogate! This practice is still happening today in a variety of forms. Because this was not God's perfect plan but His permissive plan, the pregnancy only brought trouble to the household of Abraham. Instead of solving the problem of Abraham's and Sarah's heir, it only created an animosity that split the family (Genesis 16:5). Before Ishmael was even born Hagar fled the encampment of Abraham in fear of Sarah. It is the message of the angel that we have printed above that sent Hagar back to Abraham and Sarah. (Genesis 16:7-16) I like the English devotional writer F. B. Meyer in his book Great Verses Through the Bible on this: **"Poor Hagar! No wonder that she fled. Her proud Arab independence and the sense of coming motherhood made her rebel against Sarah's hard dealings. We have often meditated flight, if we have not actually fled from intolerable conditions. Of course, when God opens a door out of a dungeon we need not hesitate, as Peter did, to rise and follow. But this is very different to flight from the post of duty."**

Why this hits home to me is the fact that in 'my great house' the Lord has made two vessels, one that has only brought honor to my home and the other that has for most of his adulthood only brought dishonor. But at the writing of this devotional he is no more living here on earth; my Ishmael passed away two months ago of liver cancer, and I am left with only my honorable vessel, but she lives in California now. I like Hagar did on a number of occasions tried to run away from Scott, but in the end I ran to him and in the last six months of his life I cared for him in my own home with my wife. Like Hagar, the Lord always sent me back into the fight for He taught me that flight is not His plan even when He places 'silver' or 'earth' (the natural man), of a vessel of dishonor in your home! I know what is expendable and so do you, if you have a troubled teenager!

Ishmael was circumcised into the Abrahamic Covenant along with the rest of Abraham's household (Genesis 17:26–27) and was loved of Abraham; just like I loved to the end my Ishmael. Despite the promise of Isaac through Sarah, Abraham still prayed for Ishmael (just like I never gave up praying for Scott) that he would be different than the harsh prediction before his birth. Eventually, Abraham's prayers were answered (as were mine) when God promised to bless Ishmael (Genesis 17:20). Not only would Ishmael become the father of a great nation (the Arab nation), but he himself would have twelve sons (Genesis 25:12–16). As a famous archer (Genesis 21:20),

Ishmael—the Troubled Teenager

Ishmael would lead a peaceful life in southern Canaan. Are you troubled with a rebellious son like I was? Is he wild and out of control like Scott was? Have you like me tried everything you can think of to help him, like I did? Have you tried prayer? For me that was all I had with my son, prayer! It worked for Abraham, and I have come to believe in the end for my son God's plan was also fulfilled. What do you think the prodigal's father (Luke 15:11–23) was doing on the porch every day before his prodigal's return and on the day the prodigal did return? I think he was praying and only the Good Lord knows how often I prayed for son!

F. B. Meyer continues his thoughts from his book Great Verses Through the Bible": "For Hagar, Sarah; for Hannah, Penninah; for David, Joab; for Jesus, Judas; for Paul, Alexander the coppersmith, life assumes hard and forbidding aspects. Sometimes the cross is a person ... We are apt to suppose that we shall get rest elsewhere. (Away from that person who haunts and harasses us!) It is not so, however. Nowhere else shall we find the path less rugged or the pillow less hard? To evade the yoke will not give us hearts ease. The Master's advice is that we shall take His yoke, and bear it as He did, remain where God has put us, till He shows us another place; and bear what He ordains and permits, even though it comes through the means of others." I don't know what your yoke was called, but for me his name was Scott, and like Hagar and Sarah, until God moves, the yoke must be worn! (God took that yoke from me on April 1, 2017, and there is a piece of me that would still like to be wearing it!)

However, the longer Ishmael and his mother stayed in the camp, the more the jealousy of Sarah increased after the birth of Isaac. (Genesis 21:9–13) Finally, God told Abraham to let Hagar and Ishmael go. Nevertheless, God never stopped watching over Ishmael. As he and his mother traveled through a waterless wasteland heading back to the country, no doubt of Hagar's birth; Ishmael almost died, and if it hadn't been for another angel of God he would have (Genesis 21:15–21). Water was found and the fourteen year old teenager (compare Genesis 16:16 and 21:5) survived to be the man God told his father that he would be. If I learned anything from my experience with my own son; sometimes you have to simply entrust them to Him (Scott survived two tours of combat duty in Iraqi and Afghanistan including being blown up three times; the last time earned him the Purple Heart!) I believe God loves our children more than we do (Psalm 127:3)! But in God's master plan for Abraham and his descendants, including Jesus Christ (Matthew 1 and Luke 3); Ishmael was expendable.

Today, you might be reading this article with a young life in your arms. As you rock and read you have often glanced into his face and wondered what he might become; what kind of man will he be? Your best hope for that child is to bring him up in the nurture and admonition of the Lord, and bring him to Christ as soon as possible. Once the child is His it is up to Him to use him for his Glory; whether a vessel of honor like Isaac, or a vessel of dishonor, like Ishmael. Let God have him early, the earlier the better, for the Father knows best, even if He breaks your heart, for in the end the child will be with Him!

19

Ezekiel—The Priest Prophet

Ezekiel 1:3

The Word of the Lord came expressly unto Ezekiel the priest, the son of Buzi, in the land of the Chaldeans by the river Chebar; and the hand of the Lord was there upon him.

Ezekiel began his spiritual ministry and legacy as a temple priest in Jerusalem in the declining days of the nation of Judah. However, Ezekiel became more famous for his prophecies than his preaching as the primary prophet of God during the seventy long years of the Babylonian Captivity. (Ezekiel 1:1–2-actually Ezekiel was among the early captives seeing that there were two other deportation before the Temple was finally destroyed in 586 BC.) Taken into captivity with the elite leadership of Judah, Ezekiel wasn't taken serious at first despite his active role among those that started to call Babylon home. His messages against the people's stubbornness and self-righteousness and his prophecies about the eventual destruction of Jerusalem and devastation of Judah were proven correct when the news arrived in Babylon that Nebuchadnezzar's army had leveled the walls of Jerusalem and burnt the holy Temple. Following those sober revelations, Ezekiel was taken more seriously and his prophesies over a 22 year period (592–570) were and still to this day are considered some of the best delivered concerning the news that a day was coming when Judah would rise from the ashes of apostasy and once again believe in the True and Living

God. (The reader ought to note that after the Babylonian Captivity Israel never had a problem with idolatry again, but other issue would arrive that Jesus would have to deal with when He came!) There was no doubt that " . . . the Word of the Lord had come expressly to Ezekiel . . . ", and there is no doubt in my mind that Ezekiel was numbered among God's 'expendable' servants!

The thing that fascinates me the most about this 'priest-prophet' is the timing of Ezekiel's trial. "Now it came to pass in the thirtieth year, in the fourth month, in the fifth day of the month, as I was among the captives by the river of Chebar, that the heavens opened and I saw visions of God." (Ezekiel 1:1) The timing of the Lord has always been interesting to me. (A case in point at the writing of this devotional I have been trying to sell a property for two years with only one half interested person that went nowhere nearly a year ago; but then out of the blue an unexpected showing and within twenty-four hours an offer that I accepted!) What has most interested me is the call to salvation or service. I have come to believe that it is not chance or circumstance when we respond to the Gospel. Two of the greatest dates of my life are June 4, 1958 (actually just two days ago I celebrated my 59th spiritual birthday), the day I gave my soul to the Lord Jesus Christ, and September 7, 1969 I gave my soles (shoes) over to the leading of the Lord. I clearly believe that like with me Ezekiel remembered the dates of God's encounters with him, when " . . . the hand of the Lord was there upon him . . . " (Ezekiel 1:2) Some have heard the call for salvation but ignored the call for service. What we must realize like Ezekiel we too are priests of God (I Peter 2:5, 9), but we are also prophets of God. We might not be foretellers but we need to be forth tellers sparing the Good News of Jesus (I Corinthians 14:1). Are you spreading the Gospel or are you hiding it (II Corinthians 4:3)?

I must stop here before I go on to my next point to also make this observation. Ezekiel, I believe, had been a faithful priest in his homeland, but it wasn't until he found a new home in a foreign land that the Lord began to speak to him; much like Daniel. As God spoke to Samuel the boy instead of Eli the high priest (I Samuel 3), God is not limited to who or where He can speak. Granted, it would seem more likely that He would talk to you in the 'city of God' verses the capital of a pagan land, but once again this is a part of God's willingness to make His servants expendable. I remember the first time I found this verse in Peter's first epistle: "The church that is at Babylon, elected together with you, saluteth you . . . " (I Peter 5:13) The

Church in Jerusalem, yes, but the Church in Babylon? Like the prodigal in Jesus' story had to go to the far country to hear God, we ask why he didn't hear the voice of God in the father's house. What the children of Israel wouldn't hear in the land of promise they would eventually hear in the land of exile. You can't tell me Ezekiel didn't preach the same message in both places? I have pastored four churches in 47 years, but what my first three flocks of 18 years wouldn't respond to my last church of 29 years have! I believe Ezekiel's life at home was sacrificed by God; his hometown ministry was expendable to God to get His servant to a place and a time where the people of God would listen to him. That is why sometimes God takes us out of our 'comfort zone' to take us to a place that people will listen. In 2010, I went to India and while there I took a mission's trip to Andrah Pardesh. In six days of preaching I saw more people come to the Lord than in the first six years of my pastoral ministry. Sometimes we have to be willing to see our time and our home expendable for the ministry of the Lord.

Another thing that interests me about Ezekiel's call was the year. It was in the 'thirtieth year'. Have you ever considered numbers in the Bible as inspired as letters? Let us use thirty as our example. Did you know according to Jewish tradition that a Levitical priest could only start his ministry after the age of 30? (Check Numbers 4:3, 23, 30, 35, 39, 43, and 47) Despite being anointed the next king of Israel at a young age David would only begin his kingship at the age of thirty (II Samuel 5:4). Jesus didn't begin his earthly ministry until He was about 30 (Luke 2:23), why all those seemingly wasted years? We know from Jesus' childhood He was already smarter than the wisest of Israel (Luke 2:46–47)! I believe that Joseph was the Old Testament type of Jesus, a young man that received visions concerning his important position in the future at seventeen, but like the others didn't start that ministry in the court of Pharaoh until he turned thirty (Genesis 41:46). To which we can add, the visions of Ezekiel only happened when he turned thirty! I believe there is a divine timetable for us as well. Each of us has been placed on this planet for a divine purpose, a holy plan; to fulfill a specific providence of God, a task of the Almighty to perform. Another prophet, a contemporary of Ezekiel, Jeremiah (remember while Ezekiel preached and prophesying in Babylon Jeremiah was preaching and prophesying in Jerusalem) was told this of the Lord: "Before I formed thee in the belly I knew thee, and before thou camest forth out of the womb I sanctified thee, and I ordained thee a prophet to the nations." (Jeremiah 1:5) What was true of Jeremiah I believe was true of Ezekiel and us. Jesus taught us: "But he that receiveth seed into the good ground is he that hearth the Word, and understandeth it which also beareth fruit and bringeth forth . . . some thirty . . . " (Matthew 13:23) Are you in the 'thirty' club?

Perhaps today you are frustrated because your ultimate purpose in life has not yet been revealed, and that God has seemingly put certain years of your life in His expendable ben! Remember, Jesus understands for He also lived those years in Nazareth. God has saved you but he has yet to call you; wait on Him (Isaiah 40:31). My final word to you is follow Ezekiel's lead and continue to do your duty, wherever you are now; be faithful, but prepare for that adjustment, God's timing; expendable to God is not wasted!

20

JOHN—THE GREAT "GREATEST"

MATTHEW 14:10
And he sent, and beheaded John in the prison.

IT WAS JESUS WHO SAID: "Verily, I say unto you, among them that are born of woman there hath not risen a greater than John the Baptist . . . " (Matthew 11:11) John though great in the eyes of the Lord was seen as least in the eyes of his enemies. It has long disturbed me that what God calls a treasure in humanity mankind often calls trash! John's generation should have been rejoicing and praising the Good Lord to have John numbered among their generation, yet John's own generation had him arrested and eventually murdered, but we should not be surprised by this seeing that same generation had the Son of God arrested, tried, convicted, and crucified! When a generation has the honor and privilege of having two of the greatest figures in history in their midst you would think they would deal with them a bit better, but even 'the best of the best', 'the greatest of the great' are expendable to such a generation. In our study of the 'expendable', we have clearly been shown in Scripture that God is willing to sacrifice His best, even the 'greatest' to His ultimate plan and purpose.

John's entrance into this world was private, but powerful: "For he shall be great in the sight of the Lord . . . and he shall be filled with the Holy Ghost even from his mother's womb and many of the children of Israel shall he turn to the Lord their God." (Luke 1:15–16) I would note after my first paragraph on John that not everyone in his generation turned on him, but their admiration wasn't enough to save him. I also thought if John would have been born in this generation the abortionist would have had a crack at him from the first doctor's visit. Surely Elizabeth was too old; the life of the mother and all that! It is still amazing to me that so called civilized man sees babies as expendable, something God sees as precious (Psalm 127:3). Later while still in the womb of Elizabeth it says: "And it came to pass that when Elizabeth heard the salutation of Mary, the babe leaped in her womb." (Luke 1:41) This is another verse in the Bible that proves that there is life before birth and that a babe can react to the outside world while still in the world of the womb. When I ponder on such stories of the Bible, check out Jeremiah 1:5, I wonder how many Johns and Jeremiahs the world has slaughtered? Only eternity will tell and only God know what invention, what miracle cure, and what great act would have been performed if mankind would have allowed them to live.

John's exhortation to his world was dramatic, but demanding: "O generation of vipers, who hath warned you to flee from the wrath to come? Bring forth therefore fruits meet for repentance." (Matthew 3:7–8) The Pharisees had turned Judaism into a works base religion. And to King Herod, the most powerful man in the land he said: "It is not lawful for thee to have her!" (Matthew 14:4) Herod had taken his brother's wife, Herodias, to be his wife. John's preaching was scriptural and sound, but people living in sin and rebellious against the purpose of faith got upset with John's sermons. The common people loved him and respected him, but the powerful started plotting from the beginning. John turned off the Pharisees and the politicians, but the people flocked to the Jordan to hear his messages and to be baptized by him. Even his cousin Jesus showed up one day. Where are the Johns today in this politically correct atmosphere? Who is demanding spiritual accountability to those who will take lightly their martial vows? Such sermons might not be popular but they are profound in the light of the Scriptures!

F. B. Meyer, the English devotional writer, writes in his book "Great Verses Through the Bible" on the need of a modern John with these words: "The Evangelist is found of the present tense, 'cometh'. Yes, these records are true to all time. You tell me that they happened 19 hundred centuries ago. Certainly but they happened yesterday, and are happening today. Remember that He is the same yesterday, today and for ever. He was, and is, and is to come. Christ was born into the world, but He is always being born in the hearts of men in regeneration. John preceded and announced His advent in

John—the Great "Greatest"

the wilderness of Judaea; and he is always preparing His way into the hearts and lives of men. It is doubtful whether Jesus ever comes into the heart of mature manhood without the precious work of a John the Baptist. Of days of conviction of sin, of remorse, of repentance, we may truly, say, 'in those days cometh John the Baptist'. John the Baptist is sadly needed today. Much of what we call Christianity is but christianized heathenism. It glozed over covetousness, luxurious self-indulgence, compliance with fashion and worldliness; it admits into its high places men who thrive on the oppression of the poor; it condones the oppression of the native races, the sale of opium and spirits, the shameless traffic of impurity; it rears the ideals of the world in the place of the changeless cross of the slain Christ with its divine sorrow and blood. Ah, we need that John the Baptist should come with his stern words about the axe, the winnowing fan, and the fire. Nothing less will avail to prepare the way for the new coming of Christ. Each age has had its John the Baptist; now St. Bernard; now Savonarola; now John Know, with sonorous, ringing voice the herald has prepare the way of the King: 'He cometh to judge the world.'" Will you be a John in your generation?

John's exit from this world was sudden, but sorrowful: "And his head was brought in a charger, and given to the damsel: and she brought it to her mother." (Matthew 14:11) From a preacher to a 'present'; John's life ended as a gift to a sensual girl provoked by a vengeful mother. Like Naboth, John was sacrificed to the world; expendable. Truly Paul wrote of such men with these classic words: ". . . of whom the world was not worthy." (Hebrews 11:38) When Jesus heard about John's death it simply says He ". . . departed thence by ship into a desert place." (Matthew 14:13) Not only had Jesus lost a family member, His forerunner, but perhaps a forewarning of His own demise in just a few short years! In God's perfect plan of redemption there was the need for the 'best', the 'greatest' to be sacrificed. We often overlook the price John paid in this plan because of the magnitude of Christ's death. If Jesus was 'expendable', then the greatest of men are also expendable. Jesus taught us: "If ye were of the world, the world would love his own, but because ye were not of the world, but I have chosen you out of the world, therefore the world hateth you." (John 15:19) Herodias hated John because of his famous sermon and the Pharisees hated John for his rebuke of them and in the end the Almighty allowed the world to have its revenge, but who in the end will get the last laugh? (Psalm 2:4)

We end this expendable devotion with recognition that we are no friend of the world. That it is so important that we realize even the best of us, even the greatest among us will be despised by the world and if it is in God's purpose the world might mistreat us, abuse us, and for some of us even kill us. Anyone that crosses the world might run afoul of the ax, and the ax might fall unexpectedly when we less expect it. What I found most interesting in the story of Herod is Herod's reluctance to kill John (Matthew 14:1–5, Mark 6:20). Even when you have the support of the world sometimes that is not enough to keep you out of the category we are calling "expendable"! For when the world sees you as expendable and the Lord know you are expendable then you will soon be expendable!

21

JOSHUA—THE SOLDIER SHEPHERD

EXODUS 17:9

And Moses said unto Joshua, choose us out men, and go out, fight Amalek: tomorrow I will stand on the top of the hill with the rod of God in mine hand.

JOSHUA FOR ME IS THE perfect example of the man of God who is willing to do whatever he is asked to do, not matter the cost or expense. For men like Joshua everything is expendable in the service of the Lord, even at the risk of one's own life.

The brilliant, God-inspired, military genius of the Canaanite campaign actually got his soldiering start in a hastily prepared battle against an experienced, war-like people called the Amalekites in a desert place called Rephidim (Exodus 17:8). Exodus 24:13 tells us that Joshua started out as Moses' servant, the deliverer's righthand man if you will; a faithful steward that Moses trusted and could call on at a moment's notice. That day of crisis arrived with a chance encounter with the Amalekites on the road to Canaan. When Moses needed a message to be delivered he sent his mouthpiece Aaron (Exodus 4:14–16), but when Moses faced his first military battle he called on Joshua. Joshua must have proven to Moses that he would carry out his instruction to 'the letter of the law', no matter what!

When Moses needed a solitary companion to accompany him up Mount Sinai Joshua went with him, and while the nation defiled them, including Aaron, at the base of the mountain Joshua patiently waited his master's return. Interestingly, when Moses and Joshua were coming down from the mountain with the Ten Commandments the noise of partying and banqueting to Joshua was as " . . . a noise of war in the camp." (Exodus 32:17) I feel that this tells us that Joshua was a military man at heart; he was created to led men into battle, and he was always ready for a fight, as we ought to be (I Peter 5:8). Such vigilance costs something, but in the day of battle such alertness might be the difference between victory and defeat! How ready are you to take up spiritual arms and fight?

When Moses needed a spy from the tribe of Ephraim to search out the Promised Land, Joshua went for him, and while the other spies, with the exception of Caleb, brought back an evil report Joshua encouraged the people with his best friend Caleb to obey God and March in and lay claim to Canaan. Joshua was ready to fight then and there (Numbers 14:6–9) for his piece of the land. Most men like Joshua have a partner like Caleb to stand in a difficult day, in a day of battle. It doesn't tell us that Caleb was at Rephidim, but I can't imagine him not being there, back to back with Joshua in the fight. In that relationship I am reminded of an article I read many years ago written by Mrs. Charles E. Cowman under the title of "Martyrs of Monotony". We remember that despite their desire to go up and possess the land that instead Joshua and Caleb had to endure 40 years of wandering before they could fight for their 'Promised Land'. Cowman writes: "In a small chapel at a Midwestern university there is a small painting of two hands raised in prayer. As you look at it, the picture seems very simple, but it tells a fascinating and inspiring tale that reaches back to the year 1490. In France two young woodcarving apprentices had often confided in each other their desire to study painting. However, such study required a far greater supply of money then they possessed, for Hans and Albrecht were practically destitute. Finally, they hit upon a solution-let one work and earn money while the other studied, then when the fortunate one became rich and famous he would in turn help the other. While Albrecht went to Venice, Hans sweated away as a blacksmith. As quickly as he received his wages, he would send them to his friend. The weeks stretched into months, the months into years, and at last Albrecht returned home to his native land-an extraordinary master-a rich and renowned painter. Now it was his turn to help Hans. The two men met in joyous reunion, but when Albrecht looked at his friend, his eyes filled with tears as he discovered the full extent of Han's sacrifice. The years of hard and heavy labour had

Joshua — The Soldier Shepherd

calloused and bruised his friend's sensitive hands. His fingers would never be able to handle a painter's brush. In humble gratitude, that distinguished artist, Albrecht Durer, painted a portrait of the work-ridden hands that had toiled so that he might develop his talent-he captured the full significance of the words of Jesus in Luke 24:40: 'He showed them His hands.'" I believe Caleb and Joshua had such hands!

When Moses needed a shepherd to take over the leadership of the nation Joshua was chosen, and while the rest of their generation died off, Caleb and Joshua walked on through those years wandering with a new generation that they could bring up in the things of the Lord. Joshua stayed alive not only to finish that agonizing trip, but to Passover the Jordan in command of the Lord's armies and win every battle he fight but one (remember Ai-Joshua 7). Joshua was possessed by a Spirit-courage on the battlefield that few ever possess. David seemed to have such courage, but rare are they. Joshua's theme song I believe were these lines from an old Church hymn: " **. . . would I (he) be carried to the skies on flowery beds of ease, while others fought to win the prize and sail through bloody seas . . . ?**" (Joshua 12:7–24) Joshua sacrificed the heart of his life; saw as expendable the bulk of his life, yet in the end he accomplished everything his heart had desired and Biblically speaking it all started with his willingness to go into battle with an untrained, lightly armed army at the command of his Master.

I have been amazed by the Battle of Rephidim for years. Consider the reason that God had taken His children the way He did: "And it came to pass, when Pharaoh had let the people go, that God led them not through the way of the land of the Philistines, although that was near; for God said, Let peradventure the people repent when they see war, and they return to Egypt." (Exodus 13:17) Joshua and his warriors that day on the battlefield of Rephidim were slaves not soldiers. There is no doubt in my mind that Joshua and his force were outmatched, overmatched, yet Joshua and his men went forth to battle believing in the power of 'the rod of God' to do what they couldn't do. Our job is always simply to go forward and allow God to clear the way. I have spent a lot of time studying this warrior and I have never found a time when Joshua was not ready, willing, and able to do the job God called him to do. It would appear from a military standpoint that Joshua and his soldiers were expendable that day, but he wasn't and neither were his men. God had a plan and all Joshua had to do was trust it and he did. Oh there were times when Joshua appeared to be losing

(Exodus 17:11), but in the end 'the battle was the Lord's' (I Samuel 17:47 and II Samuel 23:12).

Let us take a page out of Joshua's military book, for we too are in a battle; it might be a spiritual battle (I Timothy 6:11) and we might be soldiers of Christ (II Timothy 2:3–4), but the obstacles and the struggles are similar. We must go out to fight in the armor God provides (Ephesians 6:10–18) and we must follow His plan even when it seems we are losing or could lose. But we are promised victory (I Corinthians 15:57 and II Corinthians 2:14) and that no foe is too big or numerous for us to defeat (II Corinthians 10:3–4)!

22

Epaphroditus—The Courier Companion

Philippians 2:25-27

Yet I supposed it necessary to send to you Epaphroditus, my brother, and companion in labour, and fellowsoldier, but your messenger, and he that ministered to my wants. For he longed after you all, and was full of heaviness, because that ye had heard that he had been sick. For indeed he was sick nigh unto death............

Like John the Baptist (John 3:25) and Jesus (Matthew 10:1), I believe the Apostle Paul had disciples. Certain men who followed the Christ by following Paul (I Corinthians 4:16 and 11:1), and certain women that assisted Christ (Luke 8:1-3) in His ministry, so too with Paul he had certain women that helped him (Romans 16:1). One of these followers of Paul who followed Jesus was a man by the name of Epaphroditus; a name which means "lovely". This little known disciple had a lovely testimony and by all records was a lovely companion of Paul, but even this lovely man seemed expendable in Paul's work for the cause of Christ! Before we write about the event that almost took his life I think it would be profitable for us to learn a bit more about Epaphroditus.

Though Epaphroditus is only mentioned in one book of the Bible, Philippians, the characteristic mentioned about him are noteworthy:

1. There was Epaphroditus the saint. Paul called Epaphroditus " . . . my brother . . . " (Philippians 2:25) This is one of the endearing description of the Church; our 'brotherhood in Christ' (I Peter 2:17) along with 'bride' (Ephesians 5) and 'body' (Ephesians 1) and 'building' (Ephesians 2). Christ came to create a brotherhood of believers and that institution the Apostle Paul developed with men like Epaphroditus. Do you act brotherly towards your fellow Christians?

2. There was Epaphroditus the servant. Paul called Epaphroditus " . . . my companion in labor . . . " (Philippians 2:25) Paul had a great relationship with his disciples, but it wasn't a master and servant relationship as the word applies. Paul was a servant too often calling himself a 'bond slave to Christ' (Romans 1:1). Epaphroditus and the others were just 'fellowlabourers' (I Thessalonians 3:2) together with Paul. It is important that we understand the teaching of I Corinthians 3:6-9 today!

3. There was Epaphroditus the soldier. Paul called Epaphroditus his " . . . fellowsoldier . . . " (Philippians 2:25) Paul would never let his readers forget that their commission was a military calling. Paul wrote to his young warriors with terms like ' . . . war a good warfare . . . " (I Timothy 1:18) and ' . . . fight the good fight of faith . . . ' (I Timothy 6:12) He described the Christians armor (Ephesians 6:10-18) and the kind of soldier each needed to be (II Timothy 2:3-4). Are you?

4. There was Epaphroditus the sent messenger. Paul called Epaphroditus " . . . your messenger . . . " (Philippians 2:25) This tells us that probably Epaphroditus carried Paul's letter to the Philippians from his prison cell in Rome (remember Philippians is considered one of Paul's prison epistles) just like Titus carried Paul's letter to the Corinthians (II Corinthians 8:23). We often forget that we are God's messengers carrying the Good News to our family and friends!

5. There was Epaphroditus the supplier. Paul called Epaphroditus the one " . . . that ministered to my wants . . . " (Philippians 2:25) The only other place Epaphroditus is mention in Scriptures it says: "But I have all and abound I am full having received of Epaphroditus the things which were sent from you." (Philippians 4:18) Epaphroditus was a courier from the church at Philippi and seemingly stayed on to become a companion to Paul. Are you supplying the needs of others?

Epaphroditus — The Courier Companion

6. There was Epaphroditus the sick. Paul called Epaphroditus the one that " . . . had been sick . . . sick nigh unto death . . . " (Philippians 2:26–27) Seemingly while ministering to Paul for the Philippians Epaphroditus got ill and nearly died. Do ministers of God working for God get sick and almost die? No worker for Christ is immune from earthly illnesses. I have had great health for most of my life, but even I have had the occasional sickness, yes, even one that almost took my life!

7. There was Epaphroditus the survivor. Paul called Epaphroditus the one that " . . . God had mercy on him; and not on him only, but on me also, lest I should have sorrow upon sorrow." (Philippians 2:27) Each time we face the sickness of a saint we never know how the Good Lord is going to answer our supplication for them. This is where the doctrine of 'expendability' comes in. Paul was glad that God chose to show mercy both on Epaphroditus and Himself.

The story of Epaphroditus reminds me of an article I read once in Mrs. Charles Cowman's devotional, "God After All", and I quote: "In the Talmud there is a story of a peasant worker who fell in love with the daughter of his wealthy employer. She returned his love and, despite her father's violent objections, married him. Aware of her husband's ardent love for learning, she insisted that he go to the great rabbinical academy at Jerusalem to slake his intellectual thirst. He studied for twelve years while she, disowned by her family, suffered in poverty and loneliness. Though still eager for advance studies, he returned home. When he reached the front door of his house, he overheard his wife saying to a neighbor that even though the pain and separation seemed more that she could bear, she hoped and prayed that he would return to the academy for further study. Without a word to anyone, he went back to school for twelve more years of study. Once again he returned with determined footsteps back to his native village, but this time all Palestine was singing his praises as the most brilliant and scholarly mind of his generation. As he entered the market place, he was caught in the crowd of a reception committee that had gathered to honor their native son. While the people were pressing about him, he saw a woman, her body bent, her face wrinkled, desperately trying to break through to reach him. Suddenly he realized that his prematurely old woman, whom the milling crowd ignored and pushed back, was his beloved wife. 'Let her through,' he shouted. 'Let her through. It is she, not I, whom you should honor-she sacrificed while I studied. Had it not been for her willingness to work and wait, to serve and suffer, I would be today a peasant laborer and not Rabbi Akeba!'"

I am convinced that Paul had a variety of disciples like Epaphroditus who were willing to serve him and the cause of Christ no matter the cost. Like the lady of Cowman's story, behind the famous and the fortunate are those willing to sacrifice and suffer, to labor hard and long that others might fulfill their purpose. Expendable falls in a number of ways into the life of a servant like Epaphroditus or the wife of Rabbi Akeba. What I like best of Epaphroditus' story is how Paul ended it: "I sent him therefore the more carefully, that, when ye see him again, ye may rejoice, and that I may be less sorrow. Receive him therefore in the Lord with all gladness; and hold such in reputation: because for the work of Christ he was nigh unto death, not regarding his life, to supply your lack of service toward me." (Philippians 2:28–30) Expendable people don't regard their own lives, but see the service of God the higher calling; we ought to respect them!

23

Jarius—The Requesting Ruler

Mark 5:22–23

And, behold, there cometh one of the rulers of the synagogue, Jarius by name: and when he saw Him, he fell at His feet, and besought him greatly, saying, My little daughter lieth at the point of death: I pray Thee, come and lay Thy hands on her, that she may be healed; and she shall live.

SINCE CHILDHOOD I HAD KNOWN the story of Jarius, the leader of the local synagogue in the large fishing village of Capernaum on the shores of the Sea of Galilee. As a child myself hearing this story in the Junior Church of the First Baptist Church of Perham Maine, I was moved by Jarius' love for his dying child; little realizing that a day would come when I was the father and it was my son not my daughter dying! As I grew older and became a preacher of the Gospel, I loved to tell this favorite boyhood story about Jesus and Jarius and the great example of faith this father showed. I began to realize over the years that Jarius was the answer to most dilemmas people face when they come to the end of their rope with only one hope: Jesus! But that story changed in its importance and prominence on October 30, 1983 when something happened in my family after the reading of this familiar story one more time. This time my congregation was my own immediate family: my wife Coleen, my six-year old son Scott, and my 44 month old daughter Marnie. It was then I began to see this concept I have been highlighting and underlining in this devotional: that Jarius' daughter was expendable!

That day in the tiny hamlet of Westfield, Maine it was like any other day in the life of a small town country pastor. It was uneventful until after the evening meal when as had become our family custom I got out a simple children's devotional for over daily reading; years before it was called "the family altar", but we simply spoke of it as our "family devotions". Ever since our two children were babies, we had practiced this daily reading of God's word and prayer. Preacher's kids from the moment of their birth, my two children were always in Church, Sunday school, and recently they had started attending a youth ministry called AWANA (approved workers are not ashamed). Needless to say, they had been exposed to a lot of Bible and prayer outside the parsonage, but Coleen and I felt it important they know of a daily communion time with God. We were not pushy as are some parents, but believed that exposure to the Word of God would in the timing of the Spirit bring the desired result: a personal acceptance of Jesus Christ as their Saviour. I never once remember asking my kids if they wanted to get saved, for my theology taught me that when the Father calls and the Spirit convicts then Jesus would convert.

As I turned to the already picked passage of Scripture for that day, the book said to read Luke 8:41–56 before a series of question were to be answered. As I opened my Bible and read again of Jarius and his problem, the story rolled off my tongue if not out of my heart. I will admit that I was simply going through the motions because of the knowledge of the story, like we often do when we vainly repeat the Lord's Prayer. After the story and questions I was about ready to say: "Let's Prayer!" when my little daughter turned towards me and asked: "Bubby (my daughter's name for me) may I get saved like that little girl?" To my surprise and my wife's shock, we at first were stunned by Marnie's question. She seemed too young, too small to ask 'the world's greatest question'! The atmosphere in the parsonage of the Calvary Baptist Church turned heavenly as the reality of Marnie's question sunk in. Everything was forgotten as my wife and I explained the way of salvation, the why of salvation, and the who of salvation. Our concern was done, could a three year old truly understand about salvation, but she prayed the sinner's prayer and we cried, and then to our eternal joy Scott said: "Can I too?" The first sign of Marnie's salvation was she would lead her older brother to a saving knowledge of Jesus.

Jarius—The Requesting Ruler

I can hear those, as with the crowd at Jarius' house laughing (Luke 8:53). I know some think that children don't have the capacity to fully understand about salvation, but I was a child of seven when I did it, but three? That day my wife and I talked a lot about what had happened around the family table, but were determined to support Marnie's act of faith and see if it would stick, stay! At the compiling of this devotional I am 66 and my daughter is 37. I have watched her carefully for 34 years and I think the verdict is in whether or not a three year old can find Christ. By the time Marnie was eight she wanted to be a missionary and was leading children to Christ while I was camp preacher at a camp in Canada. By 16 Marnie was on the missionfield in Nigeria with a missionary couple from our Church. Through her teen years Marnie was a summer missionary for Child Evangelism Fellowship in Maine and Canada. Marnie also took a summer to go to Togo West Africa and then off to get her undergraduate degree at Lancaster Bible College in Pennsylvania. After college she was a missionary to Slovakia with Crossworld Missions for three years before returning to the states to get her Master's at Dallas Theological Seminary. Graduation in 2014 and getting married to another DTS graduate, Marnie has never once in those years since that Jarius moment strayed from the faith she claimed that day, and now we know why she lead her brother to Christ that day!

I mentioned the Jarius' story has two meaning for me. There is the connection of that story with my children's salvation, but just nine months ago I was pleading with Jesus to heal my son who had come down with a terminal illness (stage four livers and lung cancer). Since that spiritual connection in 1983, Scott and Marnie have been more than close; a family closeness but also a spiritual closeness. We all were devastated by the news Marnie flying in from California to be with Scott in North Carolina. My wife and I drove down from Maine. Jarius' daughter wasn't saved from a terminal illness and neither was my son, Marnie's brother. Note again the faith of this man, and I believe we had faith to believe, but Jarius' daughter still died, just like Scott finally yielded to the terrible disease attacking his body on April 1, 2017 (he only lived six months after his diagnosis). Most fail to see this part of Jarius' story. We too often focus on the resurrection, but fail to see that in Jesus' dealing with the woman with the issue of blood the delay resulted in the death of the daughter; must like what happened with Jesus' good friend Lazarus (John 11). Sometimes even children are expendable to the plans and purpose of God. Some say my boy died but wasn't resurrected, but I chose to believe that his resurrection just hasn't happened yet! (I Thessalonians 4:13–18)

Parent, it is never too late. Your children are already dead according to Ephesians 2:1. We all need to hear and heed Jesus' words to Jarius: **"Fear not; believe only, and she shall be made whole."** (Luke 8:50) The healing of Jarius' daughter was a physical miracle, but the healing of my daughter and son were a spiritual miracle. I love these words from the pen of John Peterson found in his classic hymn: It Took A Miracle-**"It took a miracle to put the stars in place, it took a miracle to hang the world in space; but when he saved my soul, cleansed and made me whole, it took a miracle of love and grace."** The key is simply bringing your children to Christ or Christ to your children! How important is this? One never knows how long your children will live!

24

NADAB—THE DISQUALIFIED DUO

LEVITICUS 10:1-2

And Nadab and Abihu, the sons of Aaron, took either of them his censer and put fire therein, and put incense thereon, and offered strange fire before the Lord, which He commanded them not. And there went out fire from the Lord, and devoured them, and they died before the Lord.

NADAB WAS THE OLDEST SON of Aaron, (Exodus 6:23) and by virtue of the law of God and the principle of the first born, heir apparent to the 'high priest' position after his father's death. Yet like so many other 'first born' sons of the Hebrew patriarchs; his disobedience disqualified him from attaining to that high office making him expendable in the eyes of God. Nadab's brother, Abihu, was next in line, but like his older brother he too was disqualified giving us a double illustration to the same spiritual lesson.

During the formable years under his father (Aaron) and uncle's (Moses) tutorage, Nadab seemed to have a promising career before him. He was numbered among the privileged few that were called of God to worship Jehovah at Mount Sinai ' . . . **afar off** . . . " (Exodus 24:1) Later, along with his three brothers and father, he was consecrated to the priesthood of the Levitical Worship System (Exodus 28:1). A priest with the potential of becoming the 'high priest' Nadab seeming had all it would take to make him highly successful in the new religious order created and ordained by God Himself, yet somewhere along the line something went terribly wrong.

Nadab falls into the same category as Esau and Reuben. All three were the firstborn sons of famous fathers. Esau was the first born son of Isaac (Genesis 25:25–26), and Reuben was the first born son of Jacob (Genesis 29:32). In those days not only did the firstborn son inherit a double portion in the inheritance, but they automatically became the priest of the family. When God ordained the tribe of Levi to become the priests of the nation, not only was Nadab the priest of his family but one day would be the priest of a nation! Nadab, Reuben, and Esau were also considered the political leaders of their families. Despite having the rights to all these honored positions all three men fell far short of attaining them. For Esau it was his despising his birthright that disqualified him from accomplishing what his father wanted him to achieve: "Then Jacob gave Esau bread and pottage of lentils; and he did eat and drink, and rose up, and went his way: thus Esau despised his birthright." (Genesis 25:34) For Reuben, it was the defiling of his father's bed that disqualified him for taking the leadership role in the family of Jacob: "And it came to pass, when Israel dwelt in that land, that Reuben went and lay with Bilhah his father's concubine; and Israel heard it." (Genesis 35:22) Nadab's mistake is printed in the two verses I have shared above. I would also have you note just how cheaply these men threw-away the wonderful opportunities they had: a cup of soup, a one-night stand, and a strange ritual! Most miss out on some wonderful blessing as cheaply. What is so tragic about Nadab's fatal error is that it cost him his life and the life of his younger brother.

Nadab and his brother Abihu broke one of God's fundamental laws (Exodus 30:9) by using unauthorized practices in the worship of Jehovah. God was specific in His methods and means of service, and anything else would not do. Nadab was like Cain who sought to bring God another kind of sacrifice, other than what God had specifically commanded him and his family (Genesis 4:3). It comes right down to the age old problem of " **. . . every man did that which was right in his own eyes."** (Judges 21:25) Cain sought to sacrifice as he wished too, and Nadab and Abihu sought to worship God as they saw fit. Esau sought to decide as he wished, and Reuben sought to live like he wanted too. When it comes to the ways of God we must do has He wishes not as we want. Remember how Isaiah records God's ways: " **. . . neither are your ways my ways saith the Lord. For as the heavens are higher than the earth, so are my ways higher than your ways . . .** " (Isaiah 55:8–9) When we decide to go our own way or do our own thing in the plans and purposes of God there is a terrible price to be paid. Cain became a fugitive. (Genesis 4:12) Esau became hated by God. (Romans 9:13) Reuben was cursed. (Genesis 49:4) And Nadab and Abihu died a horrible death. (Leviticus 10:1–2)

I like the way that Herbert Lockyer outlined in his book "All the Men of the Bible" (Zondervan Publishing House 1958) the transgressions of Nadab and Abihu: "Ellicott says that the sin of Nadab and Abihu was of a complicated character and involved and consisted of several acts of transgression: 1) they both offered unauthorized fire. Their vessels had to be filled with holy fire from the altar, which was always burned to be used in burning incense (Leviticus 9:24, 16:12; Revelation 8:5). Instead they used common fire-fire of their own creation. Here we have a striking illustration of the use of carnal means to kindle the fire of devotion and promise. 2) Each took his own censer and not the sacred utensil of the sanctuary. If we worship God, we must worship Him in His way (John 4:24-in Spirit and in Truth). Nadab and Abihu typify the 'will-worship' which Paul warns against, which often has a " . . . **show of wisdom and humility . . .** " (Colossians 2:23) 3) they presumptuously encroached upon the function of the high priest who alone burnt incense in a censer (Leviticus 16:12–13; Numbers 17:11). The ordinary priests only burnt it on the golden altar in the holy place (Exodus 30:7–8). Korah and his company were an exception since it was ordered by Moses for a special purpose (Numbers 16:6–25). The sin of Nadab and Abihu was a daring assumption of the mere nature, aided by religious ordinances and ecclesiastical position to enter the Lord's presence. 4) They offered the incense at an unauthorized time, since it was apart from the morning and evening sacrifice. They performed their duty in an irregular manner. Worship is only acceptable to God when offered as He has described (Exodus 30:9)!"

The Word of God is full of example of those that decided they would go their own way, do their own thing despite the Lord's instruction. Balaam, Jonah, Jeroboam, Lot, and Achan come to mind besides those already mentioned in this article; making them all expendable in one way or the other. When will we realize we can't do our own thing and get away with it; whether in the secular realm or the sacred realm? God has placed within His creation certain rules and regulations and any man treads at his own peril if he breaks those laws. Gravity is one of those laws and no man can walk off a ten-story building without dying. What is true in the natural world is also true in the spiritual world. Nadab and Abihu should have known better for they were instructed in the laws of dealing with God, yet they tested fate and walked boldly into the presence of God in their own way. There were rules and regulations that governed such behavior but they ignored all the rules to do it their way. Frank Sinatra use to sing: "I Did It My Way", and most of the world has taken up that philosophy, but that philosophy will not work in the Tabernacle of God. You can fight the law of gravity, but it will be enforced by this planet not matter your intent. It would do us all a world of good if before proceeding in anything dealing with God to check out His rights and wrongs and decided if we would be expendable or not. Disobedience to the simple instruction of God will eventually find you in a fiery judgment; whether in this world or the world to come!

25

Lazarus—The Blessed Beggar

Luke 16:22

And it came to pass, that the beggar (Lazarus) died, and was carried by the angels into Abraham's bosom . . . .

WHAT'S IN A LIFE? I have often pondered that question, especially when that life seemingly has not purpose or plenty. You and I have met many people in our lives whose life is empty and devoid of any accomplishments; contributing little or nothing to society; only taking and never giving back, people like Lazarus just *'. . . full of sores . . . "* (Luke 16:20) I am nearing my fiftieth year ministering to people like Lazarus; clients, residents of boarding homes, nursing homes that care for the sick and infirmed, the cripple and handicap. I have just finished 25 years visiting and ministering in a local home like this called Birchwood: a simple one story complex of about twenty souls that are totally dependent on others for there care, feeding, cleansing, and movement. Like Lazarus, some see these men and women as eye-sores, a sore-spot in the community, and the only difference between Lazarus and my congregation (I have become the chaplain, the pastor of these souls-I conduct services while they are alive and memorial services when they die) is Lazarus had nobody to help him so he begged, while many in my generation help people like Lazarus. People like Lazarus are a sore thing to look upon; even to this day few visit such people because they feel so sorry for them, or they can't stand looking at them. We don't know

Lazarus' illness, but I suspect there were oozing open sores that probably gave off a putrid odor; Lazarus didn't look good or smell good, but in Jesus' story there was a contrast to consider: "There was a certain rich man which was clothed in purple and fine linen, and fared sumptuously every day; and there was a certain beggar named Lazarus, which was laid at his gate, full of sores, and desiring to be fed with the crumbs which fell from the rich man's table: moreover the dogs came and licked his sores." (Luke 16:19–21) Lazarus had friends, but they were not human!

Have you ever pondered why Jesus brought these two to our attention? Donald Trump and Wayne Mallory! The billionaire verses the quadriplegic? The man who became President of the United States verses the man that spent the bulk of his manhood in a bed unable to scratch his own nose! I have come to believe Jesus gave us this story, some say a parable, but I believe a real life story that Jesus knew about to inform us into life's real accomplishments and achievements and what they are based upon. It is profound to me that three verses are given in the story to describe their lives, but ten verses are given to describe their afterlife. Oh, that the world might see this simple truth. We live in an age that is all about life, living, and lifestyle. This rich man would have been featured on the "Lifestyles of the Rich and Famous" while Lazarus wouldn't have even been given a space in the obituary column of the local newspaper. The primary lesson to me has been that we are not to judge the value of a life until 'the rest of the story' is told. If you would have met Job " . . . among the ashes . . . " (Job 2:8) full of sores your conclusion would have been like with Lazarus; what a waste, what a shame, what a blight on society instead of 'the greatest of all the men of the east' (Job 1:3). Lazarus who would depart to 'the friend of God' (James 2:23-Abraham) and the rich man, to " . . . hell . . . " (Luke 16:23) But for our book on 'expendable' Lazarus teaching another lesson about how God sees life. This story is a story of contrasts; the picture of a man ready to die and a man not ready to die; the difference of destinations based on life, living, and lifestyle.

The first thing I would have you note is that the rich man was buried, but there is no mention of the burial of Lazarus. I am convinced that both men died on the same day, but their deaths were extremely different. I think the rich man's five brothers and their families were there (Luke 16:28) and that departure was followed by a big funeral with plenty of friends, the who's who of the community in attendance with plenty of flowers, a beautiful pine coffin, a huge graveside service, and the Most Reverend So and So officiating. His eulogy commended him for his great deeds, his generous gifts (but he couldn't help a beggar by his backdoor), and there in a prominent part of the cemetery was a massive granite tombstone raised high over his resting place, but in contrast Lazarus died alone except for the few dog friends in attendance. Lazarus died of malnutrition, neglect, and a disease of the flesh. His body was left to rot in the sun until someone discovered it by the smell, and he was dumped in an unmarked grave in the Potter's Field (Matthew 27:7). Their contrast in life and their contrast in death was nothing to compared to their contrast in the afterlife, a life so many ignore today, refuse to believe today, but will one day be living there, but where?

For me, the key verse in this story is what Abraham said to the rich man: **"Son, remember that thou in thy lifetime receivedst thy good things, and likewise Lazarus evil things, but now he is comforted and thou art tormented."** (Luke 16:25) I have one simple question: which life was the expendable one? Now you know the full story which would you really chose: a life full of sores or an eternity full of sorrow? The end of the story tells us a whole lot about Lazarus' earthly life. Outwardly, he might have looked ugly, smelled terribly, and had poor friends, but inwardly beat the heart of a believer, a saint, a child of God. Lazarus' was a life called to suffer and he did it with grace and an eye on glory as we ought (I Peter 1:6-7). Grace Thirsten is a tiny lady who can't speak, whose body is constantly in spasms, who has been on a feeding tube for the last ten years of her life, but she knows the Lord and loves to be with God's people. How do I know? I have visited her for twenty-five years at Birchwood; baptized her about twenty years ago, and enjoys seeing her in her wheelchair in the middle of the aisle every Sunday she can make it. She has been a care for society all her life, but when death arrives the angels will be in attendance; can that be said of the Trumps and Gates and Zuchburgs of the world?

Better to face God's purifying fire now (Romans 8:18) than to face hell's fire later followed by the lake of fire. Paul teaches: "For our light affliction which is but for a moment, worketh for us a far more exceeding and eternal weight of glory." (II Corinthians 4:17) One day those of us who have been called to a life of '... sores...' will say His 'expendability' was worth every minute. Satan has blinded most to a short-sightedness that sees only the fine cloths, the fine meals, the fine living at the expense of eternity in agony verses an eternity in Glory. The tragedy for me in this story is that not all rich men end up in hell and not all beggars end up in the Arms of Jesus. How doubly tragic it is for those that suffer so much in this world will suffer more in the life to come. Our nation is in the grips of the worst drug epidemic in our history (so much for the war on drugs) and our back alleys are filled with beggars, but beggars not like Lazarus with a hope of a better life, and instead of giving them the real cure: Jesus! We are giving those clean needles, methadone, and a nice place to live. Instead of helping we are enabling them to continue on in their destructive lifestyle until death finds them and sends them straight to hell. We have even developed a new drug (Nar Can) that beings them back to the hellish life they are living; only putting off the inevitable and expendable!

26

Eutychus—The Saved Sleeper

Acts 20:9

> And there sat in the window a certain young man named Eutychus, being fallen into a deep sleep: and as Paul was long preaching, he sunk down with sleep, and fell down from the third loft, and was taken up dead.

Eutychus means 'fortunate', and it was very fortunate that Eutychus fell asleep during one of Paul's messages and not during one of my sermons. His sleep was fatal, for the fall from his third story seat killed him, yet at a moment's notice the Apostle Paul interrupted his sermon to give life back to this seemingly expendable lad: "And Paul went down, and fell on him, and embarrassing him said, Trouble not yourselves for his life is in him . . . and they brought the young man alive, and were not a little comforted." (Acts 20:10, 12) In our ongoing exploration into the Scriptures on the topic of 'expendability', I present to you a very unusual story out of the ministry of Paul. What made this young man expendable? What was the Lord trying to teach us about "expendable: too faithful to live long"? Consider with me for a moment the exhortation of Eutychus.

Our concern today is not whether you fall asleep in church during the pastor's sermon, or whether you fall asleep at the wheel or at your work station. For me, Eutychus has provoked in me a more serious warning about sleep that is clearly taught in the Bible:

Expendable

1. First, there is a spiritual sleep described in the Bible that we must arise from:

   "Wherefore he saith, Awake thou that sleepiest and arise from the dead, and Christ shall give thee light." (Ephesians 5:24) I believe that the Apostle Paul is writing here of the same death he wrote about in Ephesians 2:1. "And you hath He quickened who were dead in trespasses and sins?" People who might appear healthy and alive in the flesh can be dead spiritual. Are you still in a spiritual sleep caused by the disease called sin; the aliment called iniquity, or the sickness called trespasses? If you do not awaken soon you might find yourself in the lake of fire when you do awaken. Most of the world is asleep in their wickedness unaware of the danger they are in; dead, already condemned, and under the wrath of God: "He that believeth on Him is not condemned, but he that believeth not is condemned already, because he hath not believed in the name of the only begotten Son of God . . . He that believeth on the Son hath everlasting life: and he that believeth not the Son shall not see life; but the wrath of God abideth on him." (John 3:18, 36) Like Eutychus each of us needs someone to give us light and life, and that Man is Jesus (John 1:4–5). Spiritual sleep is a darkness that can only be awakened by the light of the glorious gospel of Christ! (II Corinthians 4:4)

2. Second, there is a spiritual sleep that even the Christian must be aware of: "But ye brethren are not in darkness that the day should overtake you as a thief. Ye are all the children of the light . . . therefore, let us not sleep as do others, but let us watch and be sober." (I Thessalonians 5:4–6) There are a whole lot of sleeping and sleepy saints today who are on the verge on being caught unawares. When I think of this warning I am reminded of one of the most amazing stories of the Old Testament that has been ignored by many a New Testament saint. The story is told in I Kings 13 and tells the tale of a prophet of God who was sent from the southern kingdom of Israel to the northern kingdom of Israel to warn against an alternative worship system being set up by the new king of Northern Israel, Jeroboam. The unnamed prophet was simply told to go north tell his message and when he was finished to get out; no talking, eating, or doing anything else. As the story is told the first part of his assignment went off without a hitch. However, no his way back home, he stopped for a rest under an oak tree. I think

Eutychus—The Saved Sleeper

he stopped for a nap and when the false prophet found him he was asleep. He was coming out of that sleep when he was tricked by the false prophet to come home with him for supper, and despite this being directly against God instruction he believed the false word of the prophet. After the meal it seemly recorded this: **"And when he was gone, a lion meet him by the way and slew him."** (I Kings 13:24) How many good men have been devoured (I Peter 5:8) by the devil because they were caught napping, their shields down, their swords sheathed, and their helmets off (Ephesians 6:10-18)? This is not a time to be sleeping!

I like what F. B. Meyers writes in his classic work "Great Verses Through the Bible" on this topic of spiritual sleep, and I quote: "We are inclined at first sight to pity this unknown prophet, and to justify his return; but as we look closer into the story, we not only discover the reason for the severe penalty that overtook him, but we are warned lest we make a similar mistake. When we have received a direct command fresh from the lips of Christ, we must act on it, and not be turned aside by a different suggestion, made to us through the lips of professing Christians. God does not vacillate or alter in the thing which proceeds from His mouth. When we know we are in line of His purpose, we must not allow ourselves to be diverted by any appeal or threat, from whosoever it may emanate. Deal with God at first-hand. The rule for determining the true worth of the advice which our friends proffer us is to ask, first, whether it conflicts with our own deep-seated conviction of God's will; and, secondly, whether it tends to the ease and satisfaction of the flesh, as the old prophet's suggestion certainly did. Beware of any one who allures you with the bread and water that are to break your fast. That bait is likely enough to disturb the balance of your judgment. When a voiced says spare thyself, be on the alert; it savors the things that be of man, not of those that be of God. Learn to deal with God first-hand. Do not run hither and thither to human teachers, or to the Church. Be still before God, and what He says in the depths of thy soul, do. His Holy Spirit shall guide you into all truth; and when once His way has been revealed to thee, go straight on, listening to no other voice, however much it professes Divine inspiration!" Some very good advice there in the area of sleepiness.

I have come to believe this advice was also given to us by the Apostle Paul as he dealt with this in the churches of Galatia, and I quote: **"I marvel**

that ye are so soon removed from Him that called you into the grace of Christ unto another gospel: which is not another; but there be some that trouble you, and would pervert the gospel of Christ. But though we, or an angel from heaven, preach any other gospel unto you than that which we have preached unto you, let him be accused. As we said before, so say I now again, if any man preach any other gospel unto you than that ye have received, let him be accursed." (Galatians 1:6–9) Despite the fact that Paul is writing of 'another gospel' I believe the precept we need in this area of being sleepy to the messages of our time is clear. The devil is on the prowl and he is looking for sleepy saints.

Which sleep are you in today? A sinful sleep or a saintly sleep; both can be very dangerous and deadly to your spiritual health. If it is a sinful sleep you need to awaken to Jesus' call. If you are in a saintly sleep you need to wake to a watchful vigilance: "And that, knowing the time, that now it is high time to awake out of sleep . . . " (Romans 13:11)

27

Goliath—The Great Giant

I Samuel 17:51

Therefore David ran, and stood upon the Philistine (Goliath), and took his sword, and drew it out of the sheath therefore, and slew him, and cut off his head therewith. And when the Philistines saw their champion (Goliath) was dead, they fled.

WE HAVE ALL HEARD THE expression: "The bigger they are the harder they fall!" The Biblical version of that popular expression is: "And God has chosen the weak things of the world to confound the things which are mighty." (I Corinthians 1:27) The classic Spiritual illustration of both phrases has to be the story of David and Goliath (I Samuel 17). In our ongoing search for Biblical stories that highlight and underline our doctrine of 'expendability', we have most studied the faithful men and women of God, but the more I read the Bible I have come to the understanding that there is another side to this precept: too unfaithful to live long! The Devil also has faithful followers; I would go so far to call them the 'Devil's Best', or in the case of Goliath, one of Satan's super soldiers! Those who sell out to Satan, sin, or self are also expendable, and Goliath was one of those instruments of Satan that had a shorter lifespan than even the people of God expected!

The Battle of Elah was almost never fought! "The Philistines occupied one hill and the Israelites another, with the valley (Elah) between them." (I Samuel 17:3) A stalemate had occurred because of the terrain, and the balanced forces. For either side to attack the other the Valley of Elah would instantaneously put the advantage in the hands of the force still on a hill. Military men have discovered over the centuries just how difficult it is to attack uphill. To capture a hilltop fortress takes for skill and manpower than to defend a hilltop fortress, or a hilltop emplacement. Saul realized this advantage so he waited for the Philistines to attack, but the Philistines decided on the same strategy. This stalemate lasted for forty days (I Samuel 17:16). However, while this standoff lasted the Philistines taunted the Israelites with their not-so-secret weapon: a super-size warrior by the name of Goliath; the Rambo of his day!

Goliath was a mountain of a man standing over nine feet tall (I Samuel 17:4). Goliath was armed with massive weapons of war, huge even for those days. Goliath's armor was impregnable to any weapon forged against it (I Samuel 17:5-7). Goliath's taunt was to bring on a one against one battle that would decide the war; the loser's nation would become the slaves of the other (I Samuel 17:8-10). The result was a further stalemate because " . . . when Saul and all Israel heard those words of the Philistine, they were dismayed and greatly afraid . . . " (I Samuel 17:11) Of course, the most logical opponent for Goliath was King Saul himself because when Saul was chosen king he was described as a man " . . . a head taller than any of the others . . . " (I Samuel 9:2 NIV) Though not as tall or probably as big as Goliath, Saul was the biggest Israelite and the most experienced and best soldier in the army of God at the time. And then there was Jonathan, the son of Saul that was also a high-decorated warrior (I Samuel 13-14), yet neither of them took up Goliath's challenge. Instead King Saul offered a bribe: "And it shall be that the man who killeth him (Goliath), the king will enrich him with great riches, and will give him his daughter, and make his father's house free (from taxes) in Israel." (I Samuel 17:25) But over a period of nearly a month and a half there was no takers. Goliath was the ultimate warrior of his day, at least by worldly standards and strategy. He was exceptionally tall, giving him an advantage in any one-on-one fight, and he was armed with an arsenal of weaponry and armor that could and would defy any missile thrown at it (I Samuel 17:5-6). Goliath was a walking tank surely there was no way he could be defeated?

Goliath had been trained as a warrior from his youth (I Samuel 17:33) which no doubt made him one of the veterans in the Philistine army. There is no doubt that Goliath had been on many a campaign and had fought in battles, maybe, a number of one-on-one conflicts. Goliaths experience

Goliath—the Great Giant

and arrogance made him the perfect intimidator and terminator! This giant from Gath singlehandedly frightened the entire army of Saul and despite the reward and the fame no Israeli soldier in the army came forward to challenge the giant, for who would go up against his massive spear, (I Samuel 17:7) his mighty sword, (I Samuel 17:51), or his huge shield (I Samuel 17:41)? It would be like attacking a well-fortified fort! So while King Saul and his generals debated and discussed their option on there well-prepared hilltop encampment, Goliath stood in the Valley of Elah day after day taunting Saul and blaspheming God. Such seems to be what is happening today in the arena of science, philosophy, and politics. Satan's giants boasting of their mighty knowledge and understanding, but as with Goliath they too can be defeated by the Bible as Goliath was defeated by a boy and though they look formable they like Goliath has an Achilles's heel.

Goliath's repeated challenged went unheeded until an unknown shepherd boy from Bethlehem came into Saul's camp. David had come simply to deliver some fresh food-stuffs to his brothers (three of them were fighting in Saul's army (I Samuel 17:13). Upon hearing the challenge for the first time David quickly stepped forward and volunteered for the fight. At first David's brothers (I Samuel 17:28) and King Saul (I Samuel 17:33) protested (Saul knew David for he had become his musician and armourbearer – I Samuel 16:14–21), but when there seemed to be no other solution to the dilemma, they let David marched off to face the mighty giant with a sling and a handful of smooth stones (I Samuel 17:46). David's frail frame and short stature was laughed at by the big guy. How we need to learn today that despite our size or status, we are just the kind of people God wants to use to confound and confront the world. David said it best when he told Goliath just before he killed him: "And all this assembly (both God's people and the world's people) shall know that the Lord saveth not with sword and spear, for the battle is the Lord's, and he will give you into my hands." (I Samuel 17:47)

After Goliath cursed David's God (I Samuel 17:43–44), he prepared to finish off this upstart with a quick spear thrust? With spear in hand Goliath stepped forward to administer the coupe-de-le-grace (the death blow) with his mighty spear. However, before Goliath could get close enough, David had already landed the fatal blow. With one sling of a stone, David's aim was perfect; missing and bypassing all those weapons and armor to penetrate through to the only exposed area on Goliath's body; his forehead. (I Samuel 17:49) The stone sunk deep stunning the great giant and in a moment he staggered and fell. As the Israelites cheered, the Philistines watched as their champion fell like a giant redwood tree crashing to the ground. Goliath was knocked out, but not dead. Lying motionless on the valley floor, an eerie silence gripped both armies as David took the sword from Goliath's sheath and cut off the giants head!

Today, there might be a giant in your valley. Stop looking at its size against your strength. Like David believe: " . . . many giants' great and tall, stalking through the land, headlong to the earth will fall...!" Goliath was expendable are all of Satan's giants! Remember, "Only a boy named David, only a little sling . . . "

28

Adam—The Immanuel Image

Genesis 5:1, 5

This is the book of the generations of Adam. In the day that God created man, in the likeness of God made he him . . . and all the days that Adam lived were nine hundred and thirty years: and he died.

I FOUND THIS STORY IN Mrs. Charles Cowman's wonderful devotional book, "God After All", under the title of "Hope Revived": "Day after day, Pierre, an infamous Parisian beggar, stood on his chosen corner and whined coins from passers-by who were generous only because of their eagerness to be rid of the repulsive derelict. The studio of a well-known artist was situated just a few feet from Pierre's station, and throughout each day the artist could be seen watching the beggar with unconcealed fascination. The day came when he could no longer resist the urge to paint Pierre's picture. He moved his easel and canvas to a position near the window and began to paint feverishly. When the painting was finished to his satisfaction, he stepped to the window, rapped to attract Pierre's attention and motioned to him to enter through the front door. Without a word the artist stationed him in front of the covered easel. With a flick of his wrist the drape fell to the floor and exposed the finished work. 'Who is it?' Pierre asked in wonderment. Slowly a grasp of recognition hissed through his lips. 'Can it be me?' he cried incredulously. 'That is the beggar, Pierre, as I see him,' replied the artist. 'If that is the man you see, that is the man I will be,' was Pierre's classic retort."

No man had a better start in life than Adam. "So God created man in his own image in the image of God created H him!" (Genesis 1:27) Adam possessed the very first breathe that God ever gave to a man. (Genesis 2:7) I have come to believe that Adam was the culmination of a series of marvellous miracles that took the Almighty six days to perform, and only one miracle would remain and that being the creation of the woman from a rib of Adam (Genesis 2:21–22). I have also come to believe that Adam was the most glorious creation of the triune God (Genesis 1:26), for in this creation God took His own imagine as inspiration! I have read for years the explanations of men on what it means to be created 'in the image of God', but all explanations have fallen short for me. Only if Adam hadn't marred that image we might understand, we might see for ourselves what it means, but sin changed everything for mankind and the perfect man was at fault. But in this chapter I am not going to focus our attention on just how Adam destroyed that image, but how that image is being restored in Adam's race. As with the Parisian Pierre, it is only when we get a good picture of ourselves, we finally see ourselves as we are, and we view the complete failure of our lost estate, or Adamic nature that we finally see that all is expendable so that we might be conformed to the image of Christ (Romans 8:29)!

In reality, the Bible is the history of Adam. Through the first man only lived 930 years of human history, in some respects Adam lives on in all of us because we all have chosen to follow Adam's example, not the original pattern that God established when He created Adam. When Paul decided to explain the theology of the depravity of man (Romans 1–5), he took his readers all the way back to Adam: "Wherefore, as by one man sin entered into the world, and death by sin; and so death passed upon all men, for all have sinned . . . (Romans 3:23) Nevertheless death reigned from Adam . . . for if by one man's offense death reigned by one; much more they which receive abundance of grace and of the gift of righteousness shall reign in life by one. Jesus Christ . . . for as by one man's disobedience many were made sinners, so by the obedience of one shall many be made righteous." (Romans 5:12, 14, 17, 19) Only in the mind of the Divine Designer could such a plan add up. It has taken a long time for man to get his head around this concept of the powerful influence of the One: the one Adam and the One Jesus who is also called 'Adam". As Paul explained to the Corinthian Church the truth of the resurrection, he went again back to Adam with this explanation: "For as in Adam all die, even so in Christ shall all be made alive... And so it is written, the first man Adam was made a living soul; the last Adam was made a quacking spirit. Howbeit that was not first which is spiritual... the first man is of the earth (Genesis 2:7), earthly: the second man is the Lord from heaven... and as we have borne the image of the earthly, we shall also bear the image of the heavenly." (I Corinthians 15:22, 45, 46, 47, 49)

Paul is explains in these verses that the real Adam was Christ. Adam was expendable as God proved that a simply created man could resist the wildest temptations of the Wicked One. Simple flesh and blood, even if it is created in the image of God was vunderable to the onslaught of the Devil. The eternal Father would have to send His Son to give the proper example and be the perfect sacrifice for Adam's race. We must be transformed from the image of Adam and be conformed to the image of His Son. As God originally created Adam in His own image; He is now recreating any who will believe in the death, burial, and resurrection (the pure Gospel-I Corinthians 15:1–4) of Jesus into the image of the Son. Adam is sometimes called 'the son of God' (Luke 3:38), but the real Son of God is Jesus. (Psalm 2:7)

When Jesus was praying His 'high priestly prayer' for His disciples on his way to Gethsemane and Gabbatha and Golgotha, He made this request of the Father: "And the glory which Thou gavest me I have given them that they maybe one even as we are one." (John 17:22) Jesus was asking for more than an image, but a nature as well. It ought to be the goal of every believer to pattern his or her life after the last Adam not the first; yet it seems the old Adam still has a great influence over us. Most are still following the old example of sinful Adam and his wife Eve. Instead of seeking to follow the new example exhibited by the Life of Christ. In a description of Christ in Paul's letter to the Hebrews he used this graphic word picture: "Who being the brightness of His glory and the express image of His Person." (Hebrews 1:3) Peter would write this: "For even hereunto were ye called because Christ also suffered for us, leaving us an example that ye should follow His steps." (I Peter 2:21) And the Apostle John would add this admonition in his first epistle: "He that saith he abideth in Him ought himself also so to walk, even as He walked." (I John 2:6) Only as we live like Christ, walk like Christ will we look like Christ to the world. As I was taught from childhood, the only Christ most people will see in the world will be the Christ they see in you!

Most of us need to ask ourselves this question today. Which Adam are we patterning our lives after? Sad to say most of us are still living in the image of our fallen, sinful father, Adam. Jesus went a step further when he told the Pharisees they were living like there father the devil! (John 8:44) Let us today so live until we come into " . . . the measure of the fulness of Christ." (Ephesians 4:13) When we finally see the old way, the old life, the old habit, the old lifestyle as expendable, and the new as acceptable, will be begin to understand the possibility of actually being conformed to the image of Christ. It is Immanuel's image we need to get back too. It was the image Adam lost for us, but it is the image God wants us to have back through the death of Christ; He is our only hope!

29

Elimelech—The Famine Father

Ruth 1:3

And Elimelech Naomi's husband died; and she was left, and her two sons.

PERIODICALLY IN THE SCRIPTURE, THE Promised Land of Israel was tested by famine. If you read carefully the Bible you will notice that God used the lack of food to try the special people He had called to do His work and to fulfill His purposes. Could these individuals trust and keep their faith in Him during such periods of crisis and catastrophe (think of Job)? I have seen in these trials the doctrine of 'expendable'!

During the days of Abraham, he escaped to Egypt (Genesis 12:10) because of a famine. His travels in that foreign land brought him great wealth (Genesis 12:16), but his character was tested and he was found to be a liar and the roots of his Achilles's heel and the beginning of his great transgressions can be easily traced to this sojourn in Egypt during a time of famine (Genesis 16:1). The promise of a constant supply of food wasn't worth the price Abraham would have to pay and in the case of Ishmael; the world is still paying today. Abraham could have stayed in the land of promise and he would have been just fine; trusting God during a famine shouldn't be expendable at any price!

During the days of Isaac, he stayed in the land but escaped to the territory of Gerar (Genesis 26:1). Like his father before him, Isaac also got into trouble by lying (Genesis 26:9), but as with Abraham blessed him despite himself (Genesis 26:12). In this story I see the great precept penned by Paul to the young man Timothy: "If we believe not, yet He abideth faithful: He cannot deny Himself." (II Timothy 2:13) God knows all too well what the value of expendability is, and so should we.

During the days of Jacob, he like his grandfather escaped to Egypt, but this time it was at the direct command of God (Genesis 45:11). There he found the son (Joseph) he had thought lost nearly twenty years before. Joseph was now prime minister of the land leading that country and the surrounding regions through a great famine. In all third famines the Almighty was able to work all things out for good (Romans 8:28) for Abraham, Isaac, and Jacob, but in the story of famine I would have us ultimately focus our attention on Elimelech, would this be the case? Does this precept hold turn for the man Elimelech who in a day of famine (Ruth 1:1) made a fateful choice, or did he?

Ruth 1:1 sets the stage for one of the most dramatic stories recorded in the Old Testament; a story historically found in the age of the judges of Israel, those men and women who ruled or judged Israel between the time of Joshua and Saul. Elimelech lived in Bethlehem (interestingly, which means 'bread basket or house of bread'-and if there is a famine in an area called the bread basket of Judah this must be quite a famine) with his wife Naomi and two sons, Mahlon and Chilion (Ruth 1:2). Perhaps, the meaning of Elimelech's son's names while reveal just how grave the situation was becoming in Bethlehem at the time of the departure. Parents in those days often gave names to their children because of the circumstances they found themselves in: Mahlon means 'sickly' and Chilion means 'pinning'. So in the time of the boy's birth and after the famine grew worse year after year, so Elimelech decided the grass was greener on the other side of the Jordan and moved his family to the land of Moab. Elimelech was simply living by the philosophy of the day: "In those days there was no king in Israel: every man did that which was right in his own eyes." (Judges 21:25) One can always question whether or not it would have been worse if they had stayed, but in the end we will never know because Elimelech moved his entire family east to sojourn during the time of famine. We can play the 'what if' game all we want, but in reality all we can judge is the decision and the result of the decision Elimelech made in a day of famine!

An early assessment of what happened in Moab would make us believe that a wrong decision had been made. After ten years in Moab (Ruth 1:4), had the famine lasted that long, or had Elimelech settled in Moab? All we know is that within ten years Elimelech was dead (Ruth 1:3), the first causality in this decision; Elimelech was expendable! Then Naomi made another wrong decision taking Moabite brides for her boys; we might not blame her but we know she was in direct violation of the Mosaic Law (Deuteronomy 23:3). Seemingly, not long after the marriages both boys die without children (Ruth 1:5). Mahlon and Chilion were the second and third causalities in this trip to Moab; expendable, but for what? What a price was being asked that the purpose of God might be fulfilled; three men expendable that Naomi and her daughter-in-law Ruth would return to Bethlehem. Three widows were all that was left of Elimelech's legacy, but there is more, the famine story wasn't quite over!

Even though Elimelech died long before he could have seen the good that was the result of his move to Moab, God was working out his Master Plan of not only the nation of Israel, but the redemption of the world. Everything in the plan of God centered on the young Moabite widow of Chilion; in the end Ruth would made up for the ten years in Moab and the three deaths. Ruth would not only bring into the world David's grandfather (Ruth 4:21–22) through her second husband Boaz, but she would also add to the links in the genealogy of Jesus (Matthew 1:5), the Saviour of the world. Great things can come out of famines if the Good Lord has sent them. When David wrote this verse in Psalm 33 was he thinking about his great-grandmother? "To deliver their soul from death, and to keep them alive in famine." (Psalm 33:19)

Perhaps, we like Elimelech only experience the hardship associated with famine, yet out of the devastation God can bring greater blessings. I feel today America is in a kind of famine described in Amos 8:11: "Behold, the days come, saith the Lord God, that I will send a famine in the land, not a famine of bread, nor a thirst of water, but of hearing the words of the Lord." But instead of getting discouraged over this prophecy, or stop preaching and teaching His words, I chose to believe that through this famine God is going to deliver a wonderful future harvest! From barren fields God is able to deliver a reaping, and from barren hearts God is able to deliver a glorious increase. Relive with me again the story of John 8. The Bible tells of a women caught in the very act of adultery. She was being used as an instrument to trap Jesus, but instead Jesus used that woman as an example of His amazing grace and mercy. She was broken by sin and battered by scandal and bruised by society. As others saw the outside only, Jesus looked deep into her soul and found someone that wanted to be released from the prison house she was in. The religious leaders of that day saw her as expendable, but Jesus saw her as redeemable! As with Elimelech's daughter-in-law, Jehovah saw something in Ruth. In those days parents chose their children's brides or bridegrooms, but as Naomi chose Ruth, God selected Ruth for a greater mission. I see a connection to these two stories when you consider Deuteronomy 23:3! Jehovah said to Ruth the same thing Jesus said to the woman: "Neither do I condemn thee. Go and sin no more" (John 8:11). Both hear the 'Magna Charta' of God's grace and were saved. No matter the cost, not matter the price, it is well worth whatever that needs to be expendable to get anyone to this place.

30

MALCHUS—THE SLICED SERVANT

JOHN 18:10

Then Simon Peter having a sword drew it, and smote the high priest's servants, and cut off his right ear. The servant's name was Malchus.

JESUS' FIRST MIRACLE IS WELL known: the turning of the water into wine at the wedding feast of Cana (John 2:11), but if I would ask you what was Jesus' last miracle, before His own resurrection, what would be your answer? Though Jesus' first miracle has gotten a lot of press (many books on it) and numerous comments in the commentaries, mainly because of its controversial nature, Jesus' last miracle before His death on Calvary is hardly mentioned in the spiritual books and scarcely preached on or shared. John and Luke alone mention this miracle in the Gospel, while the others ignore it. Perhaps, the only reason it is even mentioned by John is the fact that he . . . was known of the high priest . . . " (John 18:15) and probably knew Malchus. John must have recognized Malchus in the glow of the torches carried by the soldiers that came to arrest Jesus in the Garden of Gethsemane, yet in this last miracle (Jesus would perform some miracles after His resurrection-the fish catch on the Sea of Galilee comes to mind-John 21:11) before His death Jesus once again showed His love of His enemies **(Matthew 5:44-"But I say unto you, Love your enemies . . . ")** when Malchus' ear was expendable.

Malchus was certainly coming at Jesus as an enemy, but someone has also written: **"In overcoming an enemy, nothing is more effective than the weapon of love."** The problem was that Peter was quick to use violence to combat violence, as are most people. Malchus had to be thankful that Peter was a fisherman, not a swordsman! The tragedy is that most still react like Peter than like Christ. Verbal attacks today are vicious if not violent, and there has become a few who are advocating physical violence which is contrary to the teaching and application of Christ's last miracle.

Out of the Civil War comes a story of a soldier who had overheard General Robert E. Lee compliment a fellow officer who had on numerous occasions slandered the general. The soldier said to the famous warrior: "Do you know that the man you have just spoken highly of is one of your worst enemies?" "Yes," said Lee, "But I was asked of my opinion of him, not his opinion of me!" It seems as if the Apostle Paul believed in the very same strategy when dealing with enemies, for he wrote to the Romans: "If it be possible, as much as lieth in you, live peaceable with all men . . . Therefore if thine enemy hunger, feed him; if he thirst give him drink . . . " (Romans 12:18, 20) And could I add, if he tries to harm you and loses an ear in the fight, pick it up and rush him to the nearest hospital so that the surgeon can put it back on! Malchus should also be thankful that he was dealing with Christ and not the average Christian of today, or he probably would have lived the rest of his life without a right ear!

Interestingly, though John speaks of Malchus by name, it is actually Luke that gives us 'the rest of the story': **"And He touched his ear, and healed him."** (Luke 22:51) What Jesus would not do for Himself, Jesus did for a man that sought His life! What this did about Malchus' attitude about Jesus we are not told, but like the soldiers at the foot of the cross, the love and forgiveness of Christ towards His enemies must have had some affect. For at least for a moment Jesus changed the atmosphere from an ugly scene of violence into a peaceful calmness that only a miracle can bring to a hateful and hurtful situation. With a healing touch of love Jesus preached a wordless message to those who sought to kill Him, but unlike the soldier who went to arrest Jesus in the Temple (remember, the men who said: 'no man ever spoke like this man'), these men quickly remembered their mission and arresting Jesus they took him to the high priest's house!

Jesus' reaction to Peter's assault on Malchus was so much different than a story I once read in an Our Daily Bread article written by Richard DeHaan of the Radio Bible Class in the 1970s: "Two motorcyclists in a

Malchus — The Sliced Servant

truck stop restaurant tried to irritate a drive who was sitting alone. When the one of them dumped the trucker's food on the floor, the man quietly got up and left. The tough one remarked to the waitress, 'He sure isn't much of a man!' She paused as she looked out the window of the restaurant window and said, 'He isn't much of a driver either, for he has just ran his rig over two motorcycles on his way out!'" We laugh, but this isn't the way it ought to be and Jesus has given us a classic example of the right response when people abuse and misuse us. We are quick to say: "He deserved it! Cut off the other ear! Serves him right!" Not so with the Christ, for He answered His enemy with love and healing and prayer: **"Then said Jesus, Father, forgive them: for they know not what they do."** (Luke 23:34) Henry Bosch of the Radio Bible Hour and an author of the Our Daily Bread once put this precept this way in a poem: **"When wrongs to me from other come, from truth let me not stray. May I love those who persecute, and for them ever pray!"**

Malchus might not be a familiar name, but what happened to him in the Garden of Gethsemane is worthy to be remembered, for Jesus in His last supernatural act before Golgotha remembered Malchus' ear, so that he could not only hear, but show what a friend does to his enemies. It was written of a pastor who practiced the love of Christ before them that despitefully used him: **"to do him any wrong was to beget a kindness from him; for his heart was rich toward God. His spirituality was of such fine mold that if you sowed therein the seed of hate, it blossomed charity!"** So the next time you are cornered by a Malchus, remember, returning good for good is commendable, but returning good for evil is Christ-like, and that isn't expendable. We can't let such occasions be just an eye for an eye and a tooth for a tooth. Remember what Jesus taught in one of His first sermons: "Ye have heard that it hath been said, An eye for an eye, and a tooth for a tooth: but I say unto you, That ye resist not evil: but whosoever shall smite thee on thy right creek, turn to him the other also . . . .ye have heard that it hath been said, Thou shalt love thy neighbour and hate thine enemy. But I say unto you, Love your enemies, bless them that curse you, do good to them that hate you, and pray for them which despitefully use you, and persecute you." (Matthew 5:38–39, 43–44)

Jesus practiced what He preached and He had the ability to go a step further and not only show love but heal ears, Malchus' ear. Paul would admonition his readers in the reason for this: "Be not overcome of evil, but overcome evil with good!" (Romans 12:21)

31

MEPHIBOSHETH—THE ACCEPTED ACCIDENT

II SAMUEL 4:4

And Jonathan Saul's son, had a son that was lame of his feet. He was five years old when the tidings came of Saul and Jonathan out of Jezreel, and his nurse took him up, and fled: and it came to pass, as she made haste to flee, that he fell, and become lame. And his name was Mephibosheth.

I DON'T KNOW WHAT YOU think about accidents, but I have come to believe that there is no such thing! Oh, I know man likes to call happenstance, the unexplainable 'an accident', but if you believe the Bible it is clear that God is in charge of everything and nothing happens by chance or circumstance! I still remember the verse that set me to believing that there is no such thing as 'an accident': **"And the Lord said unto him, Who hath made man's mouth? Or who maketh the dumb, or deaf, or the seeing, or the blind? have not I the Lord?"** (Exodus 4:11) Or could I add the lame because of a fall? Why was Mephibosheth's walking ability taken from him at five? Why was walking expendable to Mephibosheth? Was it an accident or divine providence?

Perhaps, one of the most difficult circumstances of life to resolve is the crippling accident. It seems so unfair, unjust! The conditions of a sever handicap result in feelings of helplessness and sometimes hopelessness. Yet the Bible states very clearly: **"All things work together for good to them**

Mephibosheth — The Accepted Accident

that love God, to them who are the called according to His purpose." (Romans 8:28) What could be the purpose of God in an accident; an accident like Mephibosheth at such a young age? I believe the story of Mephibosheth can help with the myriad of questions that arise when someone we know, family or friend, has an accident. My younger brother Michael was involved in a serious car accident over twenty years ago that left him with severe headaches and chronic health issues to this day. Granted, it is a miracle he survived when a truck ran a red light and t-boned him. They say the only reason he survived was the big car he was in, yet he lives daily with the after effects of that accident, or was it an accident?

Jonathan's son Mephibosheth became a cripple at five. He might not have been even mentioned in the Bible if it were not for David's pledge: "And David said, is there yet any that is left of the house of Saul, that I may shew him kindness for Jonathan's sake?" (II Samuel 9:1) I believe one day David was thinking about his best friend (I Samuel 18:1–3), and he wanted to do something nice in memory of Jonathan. He had his servants search throughout the kingdom for any that had survived the terrible civil war (II Samuel 3–5) between the house of David and the house of Saul after Saul and Jonathan died in the infamous Battle of Gilboa (I Samuel 31). Mephibosheth survived the purge, no doubt because of his handicap! Someone has given us these words: **"There is no tragedy on earth that cannot further the purpose of heaven!"** I am reminded in the context of this story of the blind man in Jesus' days. Remember, the disciples of Jesus had asked "Why the man had been born blind?" (Maybe, they knew Exodus 4:11?) Jesus gave this answer to their question: "**... Neither hath this man sinned not his parents, but that the works of god should be made manifest in him.**" (John 9:3) Why Mephibosheth's accident, lameness? Maybe, so David could show kindness to his father? There is a purpose, a reason behind every accident which by definition proves that it was no accident. There is a lot of suffering and misery that comes with such an event, but it also opens a door for help and love and, yes, even hope!

Out of love for Jonathan David restored all of Saul's property to Mephibosheth. Overnight the poor cripple because one of the richest men in the land, as well as one of the most powerful men in the kingdom of David. Mephibosheth was even given one of the coveted seats at David's table (II Samuel 9:3). When Mephibosheth was setting at David's table nobody could see his lameness, for the table cloth hid his crippled legs. Years later during the rebellion of Absalom Mephibosheth's servant Zibah tried to discredit Mephibosheth in the eyes of the king by spreading a rumor that Mephibosheth had side with Absalom because Mephibosheth had no left Jerusalem when David fled (II Samuel 16:1–4), but when David was able to return to Jerusalem he learned that Mephibosheth had remained loyal through the whole affair. (II Samuel 19:24–30) So as the years passed Mephibosheth accepted the purpose of God in his life and I believe no longer saw his crippled state as a handicap, but an honor. It was because of his so called accident that he had gained acceptance in the eyes of the king. The last mention of Mephibosheth in Scripture verifies this thought to me. When David gave up the last of Saul's descendants to the Gibeonites for execution because of a sin that Saul had committed against them; a matter that had never been resolved to God's satisfaction, we read: " . . . But the king spared Mephibosheth . . . " (II Samuel 21:7) Why, his lameness?

Perhaps you have been called to endure a tragic accident that has left you or a loved one crippled in some way. Have you ever tried seeing your accident through the eyes of God? I love the music of Fanny Crosby and hers is the story of being a cripple for all of her life. As a young girl she was blinded accidentally, but living into her nineties she was a shining testimony throughout becoming the sweet psalmist of the nineteenth century Church. We must realize that men like Mephibosheth and ladies like Fanny are as much a product of God's purpose as the healthy ones, people like me. Each of us must accept God will in what we are and what has happened to us for each piece of our life He has given us our health or our handicap for His glory and our good!

Let me finish my thoughts on Mephibosheth and accidents with this great story from the pen of Mrs. Charles Cowman in her devotional book "Mountain Trailways for Youth" put out by Zondervan Publishing House (1947): "A great and majestic cathedral was the focal point of interest in an ancient city. Among other things, it was noted for a very special stained glass window. Its fame became so great that people came from far and near to gaze upon the splendor of this masterpiece of art. One day a very violent storm swept across the land, and the great window was jolted loose and crashed to the marble floor below. It seemed hopelessly shattered into thousands of unidentifiable pieces. The people were crushed by this catastrophe that had so suddenly bereft the town of its proudest work of art. They sadly gathered up the broken pieces, piled them in an old box and carried them down into the cold, damp church cellar. Sometime later, a stranger appeared at the church door asking to see the beautiful window. They told him of its fate. He asked what they had done with the fragments, and they took him to the cellar and showed him the broken pieces. 'Would you mind giving them to me?' asked the stranger. 'Take them along,' was the reply, 'They are no longer of any use to us.' Months later and invitation reached the custodians of the old cathedral. A famous artist announced the completion of his greatest work-a stained glass window. At the appointed moment, the master-artist ushered his visitors into the presence of one of the most exquisite works of art their eyes had ever beheld. They gazed entranced upon the rich tints, its wondrous pattern, and cunning workmanship. The heavy silence was quietly broken by the low voice of the artist. He said: 'This window has been made from the fragments of your shattered window!'"

32

Hophni/Phinehas—
The Scandalous Sons

I Samuel 4:11

And the ark of God was taken; and the two sons of Eli, Hophni and Phinehas, were slain.

This will be the only time in this book that I will use two Biblical characters in the same devotional. At first, I thought that I would deal with them separately, but I found in my research that you really can't separate the boys of Eli. I discovered that they are not mentioned once apart from the other; that what is said of one is said of the other. I doubt they were twins, but in life they were identical twins! And in the ultimate purpose of God, they were expendable!

"Now the sons of Eli were the sons of Belial; they knew not the Lord." (I Samuel 2:12) In our day with the ministries of the Lord Jesus Christ under attack because of the greedy, glory-seeking individuals (I Peter 5:2–3) that have entered the world of the Lord, we understand clearly the effect of a Hophni and a Phinehas on the priesthood (I Samuel 1:3). When Eli attained to the position of High Priest of the nation of Israel, he became not only the spiritual leader of the land, but the political leader as well (I Samuel 4:18). His sons were to follow his faithful footsteps; Eli had even named one of his sons after the grandson of Aaron, the first High Priest, Phinehas (Psalm 106:30–31). Eli's son however turned out much different

Hophni/phinehas—the Scandalous Sons

than he and his wife had planned. There is no guarantee that our children will turn out good; not matter how much we teach them, encourage them, or are an example to them. Hophni and Phinehas were unprincipled and unscrupulous in all their actions. You talk about a sandal in the highest levels of government and in the tabernacle! So what happened that cause them to be expendable with 'the ark of God'; another amazing reality when you consider that 'the ark of the tabernacle' was the ultimate dwelling place of God (Exodus 25).

First, Hophni and Phinehas took advantage of their position as priests in the tabernacle at Shiloh to steal from God (Malachi 3:8) by taking more than their share of the Lord's sacrifices (I Samuel 2:13–16): "Wherefore the sin of the young men was very great before the Lord; for men abhorred the offering of the Lord." (I Samuel 2:17) Hasn't this been happening today in the area of giving in the Church? So many ministers have skimmed from the Lord's treasury to build their own mansions and memorials, for selfish and self-centered things not considering the Lord's work. Like in the days of Hophni and Phinehas people have gotten sick and tired of giving to the Lord because of the mishandling and misuse of the Lord's funds by the Hophni and the Phinehas of our day. When I ponder this problem both then and now I am reminded of the admonition of the Apostle Peter in his first epistle: "Feed the flock of God which is among you, taking the oversight thereof... not for filthy lucre, but of a ready mind..." (I Peter 5:2)

Second, Hophni and Phinehas were wicked with women. (I Samuel 2:22) They did as Paul said would happen in the last days (II Timothy 3:1): "Having a form of godliness, but denying the power thereof, from such turn away. For of this sort are they which creep into houses, and lead captive silly women laden with sins, led away with diver's lusts." (II Timothy 3:5–6) So today, the preachers of lust have become headline stories. Sex and the ministry aren't new, but for each generation that must endure this shame, there is a day of judgment for them, as with Hophni and Phinehas. As I write this devotional I have just heard from my mother who is visiting with my older sister a grandson in New Mexico. I texted to see how things were going on their first weekend. Mother texted and told me their first visit to church wasn't nice because she was greeted by the associate pastor having to explain to the congregation about the pastor's resignation because of an extra-marital affair! Sound Familiar!

Despite the rebuke of their father in these matters (I Samuel 2:23–24): "Notwithstanding they hearkened not to the voice of their father because the Lord would slay them." (I Samuel 2:25) This should be a warning to all those who would follow the example of Hophni and Phinehas, and this ought to be an eye-opener to any parent that thinks that a simple rebuke can change the pattern of their children as they get older. Correction needs to come early if there is any hope, adulthood is often too late. As these two brothers faced the wrath of God in their day of judgment, so will everyone that tries to hide their sinfulness in the sanctuary of God. Man might turn a blind eye but not God!

Granted, the news that Day of Judgment was not good as Phinehas' wife went into labor. Word had just arrived at Shiloh that Israel had lost the Battle of Ebenezer (I Samuel 4:1–2) against their archenemy the Philistines. Phinehas' and his brother Hophni were dead, and the Ark of the Covenant, Israel's most sacred spiritual symbol, had been captured. The tragic news had resulted in the accidental death of the High Priest Eli, the boy's father (I Samuel 4:15–18). So within a few minutes she learned of the death of her father-in-law, brother-in-law, husband, and four thousand brave Israeli soldiers. (I Samuel 4:2) The shock was so overwhelming that it brought on labor pains and contractions (I Samuel 4:19). It was a difficult delivery and the Bible simply records: "And about the time of her death!" Phinehas' wife was also dying. The midwife who was in attendance tried to cheer the unnamed lady up by delivering the news that she had a son, Phinehas' son (a son he never got to see), but the good news wasn't good enough to overcome the bad news from the battlefront. She called the boy Ichabod (the glory is departed) because of the deaths and the capture of the ark. (I Samuel 4:19, 21–22) What is sad in such tragedies is the fact that in the midst of all this bad news their remained the best Good News of all; the ark might be gone, her husband might be gone, but the Lord was still there! God was not dead, for God is never expendable!

Mrs. Charles Cowman tells this story in her booklet, "**God After All**": "A memorable dinner was reported in London more than fifty years ago. It was given by Christopher Neville for some of the leaders of England's thought-leaders in politics, literature, finance, art, and religion. Following the dinner Dean Stanley proposed a discussion of the question" 'Who will dominate the future'? He called upon Professor Huxley to speak first. The professor arose and indicated that his opinion the future would be dominated by the nation that adhered most closely to the facts. The audience was profoundly impressed. After a moment of silence, the Dean again arose and called upon an English journalist, who was also a Member of Parliament

Hophni/phinehas — The Scandalous Sons

and President of the Royal Commission on Education. Beginning quietly, he went on to say, 'Gentlemen, I have been listening to the last speaker with profound interest and I agree with him in his premise that the future will belong to the nation which sticks to the facts. But I want to add one word-all the facts, not just some of them. The greatest fact in history,' he continued, 'is God!'" The one fact that is not expendable, but a fact that both then and now seems to be ignored!

The Bible begins: "In the beginning God . . . " (Genesis 1:1) Hophni and Phinehas ignored the God of the tabernacle they served to their bitter end. When you ignore God; when you leave Him out of your life you do it at your own peril; God isn't expendable!

33

Jephthah—The Dangerous Dad

Judges 11:31

Then it shall be, that whatsoever cometh forth of the doors of my (Jephthah) house to meet me, when I return in peace from the children of Ammon, shall surely be the Lord's, and I will offer it up for a burnt offering.

Paul wrote in his chronicle of the most famous faithful of the Old Testament these words: **"And what shall I more say? For time would fail me to tell of . . . Jephthah . . . "** (Hebrews 11:32) Jephthah is a great example and illustration of a faithful person with a fault! If you have done a study of the characters of Scriptures as I have you too will discovered that most of the most faithful had a fault, a flaw somewhere in their character, and Jephthah, the judge of Israel was no exception. If we are honest with ourselves we too must admit that no matter how faithful we have been to Christ and His cause we too have failed, but Jephthah's flaw proved fatal to his only daughter and himself. When Jephthah made a deal with God; tried to bargain a victory from God he proved that everything was expendable for a win, even though I don't think he thought through that it might be his only child! We need to be very careful when we seek something at a cost because it might just cost us our most treasured possession!

"And Jephthah vowed a vow unto the Lord, and said, if thou shalt without fail deliver the children of Ammon into mine hands." (Judges

Jephthah—the Dangerous Dad

11:30) Some of the men I have read on this call this a 'rash vow'? All I can say is that Jephthah did it with ' . . . **the Spirit of the Lord . . .** " (Judges 11:29) upon him; which reminds me that even a Spirit-filled man can show himself vunderable. I like to remind my audience that what is any different what Jephthah did then what Gideon did in asking God a sign after God promised him a victory over the Midianites? (Judges 6:36–40) Gideon wasn't rebukes by God and neither was Jephthah, so why should we. Is there something in these stories that we need to learn about God? Scriptures would later rebuke such vows in Jewish history when the wise man Solomon wrote: **"Be not rash with thy mouth and let not thy heart be hasty to utter any thing before God for God is in heaven and thou upon the earth therefore let thy words be few."** (Ecclesiastes 5:2) Was Solomon remembering the Jephthah story when he wrote this important precept?

I remember when I was a child of eight, just one year after I had given my heart to Jesus (June 4, 1958). I made a vow to God to read a chapter in His Good Book every day for the rest of my life. I was sincere and I thought it might please God, but as you can already imagine; I couldn't, I didn't, and I haven't! Though over the years from that day (nearly 60 years now) I have read the Bible through over fifty times there have been plenty of days I haven't picked up the Bible to my shame. Yes, it was a rash vow, but I believe made in the ignorance of a childish desire to please God. What I have learned over the years is this isn't the way God wants us to please Him: **"But without faith it is impossible to please Him: for he that cometh to God must believe that He is, and that he is the rewarder of them that diligently seek Him."** (Hebrews 11:6) I believe that this was the case with Jephthah as well. Jephthah didn't know Jehovah like he should, but that doesn't change the story because of these sobering words from Solomon again: **"When thou voweth a vow unto God defer not to pay it, for he hath no pleasure in fools paying that which thou hast vowed."** (Ecclesiastes 5:4) How many fools vows have you made?

The tragedy of the story is that Jephthah's daughter was the first thing that came out of his house on the day of victory over the Ammonite army (Judges 11:34) And then we read these sad words: "And it came to pass at the end of the two months that she returned unto her father who did with her according to his vow which he had vowed." (Judges 11:39) There is much debate over whether Jephthah actually sacrificed her or not, I think not. If God wouldn't allow Abraham to sacrifice his innocent son Isaac (Genesis 22), I can't imagine God allowing Jephthah to kill his innocent daughter?

I have come to believe the punishment was that Jephthah's daughter remained a virgin for the rest of her life thereby giving Jephthah no grandchildren and a legacy and an heir; a fate worse than death to a woman and a fate worse than death for a Jewish family. Read carefully Judges 11:37–40 you for I have come to believe that Romans 14:5 applies here!

For me the real debate in this story has to do with vows and what does Solomon mean when he writes: **"Better it is that thou shouldest not vow than that thou shouldest vow and not pay."** (Ecclesiastes 5:5) Compare carefully and you will see that Jesus taught a similar doctrine in Matthew 5:33–37! I feel in these verses the Bible is very clear when it comes to vowing, but if you vow God will hold you to your vow which reminds me of a story I read once in a Mrs. Charles Cowman's devotional from her devotional "Traveling Toward Sunrise" (Zondervan Publishing House 1954): "There is a fascinating legend concerning a tribe of North American Indians who roamed in the neighborhood of Niagara. Each year they offered a young virgin as a sacrifice to the Spirit of the mighty river. She was called '**the bride of the falls!**' The lot fell one year to a beautiful girl who was the only daughter of the old chieftain. The news was carried to him while he was sitting in his tent; but on hearing it, the old man just went on smoking his old pipe in complete silence. On the day set aside for the sacrifice, a white canoe, full of ripe fruit and decked with flowers was ready and waiting for 'the bride'. At the appointed hour she took her place in the frail bark. It was pushed out into mid-stream, where it would be carried swiftly towards the mighty cataract. Suddenly, to the amazement of the breathless crowd, a second canoe was seen to dart out from the river bank-in it was seated the old chieftain. He paddled with swift and powerful strokes towards the swirling sacrificial canoe. He reached it, gripped it firmly, and held fast. The eyes of the father and daughter met in one last look of love; and then, close together, they were carried by the racing current until they plunged over the thundering cataract and perished side by side. The father was '**in it**' with the child!"

Could I suggest to you that this was 'the faith of Jephthah'? I have come to believe that Jephthah would have been given the victory without the vow! But in making the vow God would require Jephthah to fulfill the vow, and I believe he did. Like the chieftain and the daughter bearing the sacrifice together, so too did Jephthah and his daughter. Jephthah's faith was in believing that God's will was the virgin life of his daughter and him no gaining any grandchildren because she was his only child (Judges

Jephthah—the Dangerous Dad

11:34). That is why we must think through a vow before uttering it. James the brother of Jesus tells the Church clearly: "But above all things brethren swear not neither by heaven, neither by the earth neither by any other oath, but ley your yea be yea, and your nay be nay, lest ye fall into condemnation." (James 5:12) The message is clear to me; stay away from vows! If you don't then in the end something will be expendable. God demands no vows, but we all make them. I think today of marriage vows mankind is failing to fulfill in society; is this the reason we have so many problems, a direct result of not keeping vows. Jephthah is not only a good example what not to do, but when you do then be faithful in the vow!

34

Manoah—The Prodigal's Parent

Judges 13:2

And there was a certain man of Zorah, of the family of the Danites, whose name was Manoah; and his wife was barren, and bare not.

Mrs. Charles Cowman writes in a book called "Harvest Secrets" (Zondervan Publishing House): "Tragedy had struck at the very heart of the British Empire-one of her favorite sons lay still in death. The Duke of Wellington, once invincible in battle, now lay lifeless in the great hall, surrounded only by those vigilant sentries who maintained their final watch. Dignitaries journeyed from every dominion and protectorate to pay tribute to their fallen hero and statesmen, and a special section was established in the great cathedral for the chosen representatives of every military unit of the vast colonial army-every regiment of every country flying the Union Jack would stand in final homage to their great man." Many years before this historical event in England a similar tribute took place in the territorial allotment for the Tribe of Dan: "Then his brethren and all the house of his father came down, and took him, and brought him up, and buried him between Zorah and Eshtaol in the burying place of Manoah his father. And he (Samson) judged Israel twenty years." (Judges 16:31) Samson, the great champion of Israel, was dead and his countrymen came to pay tribute to the prodigal son of Manoah. Little did Manoah dream at the birth of his only son just how expendable he was? An unexpected life that started

Manoah—the Prodigal's Parent

out with such promise ended so tragically. Little did I know in 1977 that I would live the life of Manoah, a life with a prodigal son; little did I know the cost of expendability?

In 2010, I had the wonderful privilege to travel to a place in Israel where I would see Zoar and Eshtaol from the archeological tel of Bethshemesh. Standing on that mount I witness the entire life of Samson as I could see into the Philistine coastal cities and the valley of Sorek (Judges 16:4) where Samson met his fate at the hands of Delilah. But instead of focusing on the life of Samson, I choose in this chapter to feel the heartache of Manoah. Manoah will always be known as the father of Samson, the strongman of Israel, but I feel he should be known for more than the father of a prodigal. Only those of us who have raised a prodigal can understand the high price a parent pays being a prodigal's parent, or a prodigal's father. Samson's mother was devastated as was Coleen, Scott's mother, and expendable is an appropriate term to use for such a relationship!

It is no little matter to raise an exceptional child, whether exceptional in a mental way or in a physical or spiritual ability. Some people feel it must have been easy to raise Jesus, but I don't get that impression from reading Luke 2:41–52! Just because a child is destined for greatness (Judges 13:5); that doesn't mean it makes it any easier on the parent of such a child. I believe as God chose carefully the parents He would entrust His Son too; He chose carefully the parents of John the Baptist and the parents of Samson. I do not believe it was by chance or circumstance that Scott, my son, was given to Coleen and I to raise. The Psalmist said it best when he wrote: **"Children are an heritage of the Lord . . . "** (Psalm 127:3), but so are parents. God gives certain children to certain parents. The pairing up of children and patents is not the result of some heavenly lottery as some seem to preach. It is not genetic roulette that determines our pairings, but the divine sovereignty of God's choosing! And as God chooses, He also knows when a child will turn out to be a wayward prodigal, and He knows it takes a special parent to deal with the exploits of a rebellious prodigal son!

When Manoah found out the details of the special child his wife was carrying, what did he do first? Celebrate because he was having a child he never expected to have? No! "Then Manoah entreated the Lord, and said, O my Lord, let the man of God which thou didst send come again unto us, and teach us what we shall do unto the child that shall be born." (Judges 13:8) Oh, that more parents would find it necessary to seek the Lord on how to raise a Samson, even when they don't know he will be a Samson. Parents read books on child rearing; they ask their parents, and go to seminaries on child care, but when was the last time they pleaded like Manoah for divine instruction? I have come to believe the manual for raising a child is the Bible, but the Bible is often the last place we look. It is the textbook for bring up a child " **. . . in the nurture and admonition of the Lord."** (Ephesians 6:4) We seek Naramore (a child psychologist when I was a young man) or Dobson (a famous Christian psychologist when we were raising our kids), but all secondary sources when the Bible is readily available. Some of their material contains the Word of God, but only the Word of God contains the advice of the Almighty, especially when you need advice for raising a prodigal son (Luke 15:11–32)!

Even when Samson became a grown man Manoah didn't stop being his father (Judges 14:3), or giving him godly advice, but prodigals don't take the advice of their fathers and thereby continue on a road that leads to an early grave! Good parents don't always raise good children, but in the Samson story we learn a valuable lesson: "But his father and mother knew not that it was of the Lord . . . " (Judges 14:4) God even has His plans for prodigals. My son Scott turned into a prodigal at 18 and when he contracted cancer at 38 he was still a prodigal. Like Jesus' parable, Scott did return to his father's house in repentance and I believe died reconciled to his parents and His God, but in the end he still died. I believe I will met Scott again in glory just like I believe I will meet Samson as well (Hebrews 11:32), but that doesn't ease the burden and frustration in life with dealing with a prodigal. Parents do the best they can with all they can, but in the end their child will choose for him or herself! We know that in the end Manoah was right and Samson was wrong, but that doesn't bring much solace when you stand before the grave of your 39-year old son and they play taps over his tombstone. (My son was a 12-year veteran of both the Iraqi and Afghani wars; serving honorably in three tours of duty!)

I am nominating Manoah and his wife as parents of the year, for their faithful raising a difficult son, a son with an Achilles' heel: strange women (Proverbs 7). The irony of Samson's story for me and my wife is that our son had the same weakness. Catch at an early age, Scott was under the power of these women almost to his dying day. I am not saying they cause his death, but I am saying, like with Delilah, they hastened his death! Despite the great good they (Samson and Scott) did in helping others and fighting battles (Scott was a decorated soldier with even a Purple Heart), each fell in the end; which brings me to the whole point of this devotional. Dear parent

Manoah — The Prodigal's Parent

of a prodigal: for years I blamed myself, or others that turned my beloved and only son into a prodigal. The more I meditated on the relationship Manoah had with his son the more I realized in his story was my story. It wasn't until Scott's story was over I could see the complete story of Samson's story in the life of my son. Any parent can raise a prodigal; it has nothing to do with parenting, it has to do with providence. God knows that even the most gifted, the best raised, the best endowed can make wrong decisions; even reject godly, parental advice. Sometimes we as parents must be willing to sacrifice our children on the altar of expendability for the divine purposes of God. Sometimes God doesn't tell us everything!

35

BARAK—THE SCARED SOLDIER

JUDGES 4:9

And she said, I will surely go with thee: notwithstanding the journey that thou takest shall not be for thine honour; for the Lord shall sell Sisera into the hand of a woman. And Deborah arose, and went with Barak to Kedesh.

WHEN WILL THE AVERAGE CHRISTIAN ever learn this classic precept from the pen of Paul: **"For the gifts and callings of God are without repentance?"** (Romans 11:29) When God called Jonah to preach against the mighty Assyrian city of Nineveh (Jonah 1:2) and Jonah decided to take a Mediterranean cruise instead, God didn't call someone else to do the job did He? God went and brought Jonah back and recommissioned him for the task (Jonah 3:2). When it comes to an individual's commission God has no substitutes, but God can give your glory or honor to another if you are reluctant to fulfill your commission on your own, for both are expendable in the light of such hesitation as we will see in the story of the soldier called Barak; even a man of faith (Hebrews 11:32)!

When it was time again (note the continual repetition in the Book of Judges) for God to deliver the Israelites from the oppressive King Jabin of Hazor, God told the judge Deborah to call for a man by the name of Barak, but upon hearing his mission Barak balked: "And Barak said unto her, if thou wilt go with me then I will go, but if thou wilt not go with me, then I

Barak—the Scared Soldier

will not go." (Judges 4:8) Most commanders-in-chief would have replaced Barak then and there, but Deborah knew Romans 11:29, or at least the concept of Romans 11:29. She had gotten her orders from God and she knew that Barak was God's man even if he was hesitant to go alone! How often did President Abraham Lincoln replace his military commanders during the American Civil War? He did it over and over again because they were not fighters; that is until he came to a man named U. S. Grant. Up until Grant most were like Barak; too cautious, too scared. Caution is not a bad virtue unless it is applied when God says attack. When God's calls us to lead the assault we must have a holy daring, a godly courage; Barak seemed to have neither!

I have come to the conclusion that Barak had Moses' problem; he didn't want to fulfill his commission alone! Moses wanted Aaron, or any Aaron and Barak wanted Deborah. Moses balked at first just like Jonah balked at first and so did Barak balk at first, but in all three stories God eventually got his man in the right place to fulfill His divine purpose. Moses eventually arrived in Egypt to deliver the children of Israel from their 400 year bondage. Jonah eventually arrived in Nineveh on time to preach the message of repentance and the salvation of that huge city. And Barak eventually arrived in Tabor in time to lead the charge that would set the army of Hazor to flight. Granted, Barak lost the honor of killing Jabin's top general, Sisera, (Judges 4:9) but he never lost his commission, and neither shall we though we all have the potential of losing some rewards (II John 8). It all depends on how much of our reward is expendable to us?

Why does God patiently put-up with people like Moses, Jonah, and Barak? Yes or even Barry (that's me)? I must admit that I over the years have balked at a few assignments. George Eliot once wrote a simple little poem about the famous violin maker Antonio Stradivari titled "Stradivarius": **"If my hand slacked, I should rob God-since He is fullest good, leaving a blank instead of violins. He could not make Antonio Stradivari's violins without Antonio."** Remember, when Gideon attacked the Midianites his three-hundred shouted: "The sword of the Lord, and of Gideon!" (Judges 7:18) and God in His wise providence has determined to use people to perform His works. God could do it alone, but He has determined to use Barak and Barry to fulfill his purpose. We are important to God and He wants to honor and glorify His name through us: "Let your light so shine before men, that they may see your good works, and glorify your Father which is in heaven." (Matthew 5:16) Ultimately, God will get the honor and glory, but part of our reward for faithful serve is also honor and glory. Barak would lose his 'honor' when he refused to fulfill his commission alone!

Doctor John Matthews, an early radio evangelist, once said on his program: "When we weary of famines and floods, pestilence and poverty, conflict and war, then these plagues shall pass into history forever. They are here because we have submitted to dread and fear. We forgot the path to prayer and the force of faith . . . God never planned any such age or hour . . . When Moses prayed, Israel was saved; when Samuel prayed, the Philistines fled in defeat . . . When Jonah prayed, a million souls were spared. It is up to us to turn the tide: man remains the deciding factor. When God predicts judgment or impending disaster, it is impossible that we may avert it? Unless we act, judgment will surely fall; unless we set up counter laws that will rush out to meet overwhelming evils, disaster will be the result . . . Someone asks: 'If God predicts or gives His Word, will not that Word come to pass in face of all men may do?' Not necessarily so . . . nothing is more harmful than the failure to distinguish between the eternal decrees of God and His conditional purposes, which we may further, or if need be prevent." Barak was a good soldier or he would never have been called and the Canaanites would be defeated, but Barak's decision to balk was ultimately for his lose not God's. God always wins, but do we? The choice is ours to decide how we will be blessed or honored depending on our obedience to God's commissions and God's orders.

When the war was over Barak co-authored with Deborah one of the most famous songs in all of Jewish history (Judges 5); study this beautiful duet, one of the most beautiful hymns of history, and you will note that though Barak hesitated at first he fulfilled the call and would be known as one that ' . . . lead . . . captivity captive . . . ' (Judges 5:12) That is a Christ-like characteristic according to the Apostle Paul in Ephesians 4:8. Barak's actions were anything but admirable at first but he would be numbered among the faithful (Hebrews 11:32) and honored in a song. Granted, Jael and her nail would attain to the most glorious verse of the song (Judges 5:24–27), but Barak would be honored for his part in the victory. So too can we be victorious in our own lives despite the occasional balk at God's call; God is determined to use you and me, despite our caution, cowardliness, and cruises: though sometimes you might have to share your victory with another, you will still be used. God's call is for you and you alone!

Let us today receive boldly God commission or recommission and get into or back into the work God has called us into, for we know that in the

Barak—the Scared Soldier

end we have this promise: **"But thanks be unto God which giveth us the victory through our Lord Jesus Christ."** (I Corinthians 15:57) Your reward might be expendable depending on how far you are willing to boldly step out: "Look to yourselves, that we lose not those things which we have wrought, but that we receive a full reward." (II John 8) But your place on the battlefield is never in doubt because your call and gifts are irrevocable. God's eternal plan requires people like Barak, good or bad. I would close with these simple lines: **"Others may do greater work, but you have your part to do; and no one in all God's heritage can do it so well as you!"**

36

Jeremiah—The Tired Teacher

Jeremiah 9:2

Oh that I had in the wilderness a lodging place of wayfaring men; that I might leave my people, and go from them! For they be all adulterers, an assembly of treacherous men.

"And Jeremiah lamented for Josiah." (II Chronicles 35:25) Jeremiah has come down through history as the 'weeping prophet' for many reasons. This lonely, sensitive Hebrew prophet had to preach and prophecy in an age of only bad news. After the death of Josiah it was a downhill spiral for the nation of Judah until they finally fell into captivity and Jeremiah had to deliver every devastating prediction. Judah's decline both spiritually and politically came at a tremendous cost personally to the loyal Jew because his messages and sermons were seen by his own people as treason. Towards the end, Jeremiah was harassed and hounded and even hunted by those who saw Babylon as the enemy and Jeremiah as their spy (Jeremiah 27:17). At the lowest point in his life the aged prophet was lowered into a muddy cistern to die, and if it hadn't been for a friendly Ethiopian he would have died. Despite the persecution and the occasional trip to prison, Jeremiah kept on delivering: **"*This saith the Lord!*"** (Jeremiah 27:2). Jeremiah is a wonderful example of the cost of being 'expendable' to God!

Perhaps, the most mournful book ever written is Jeremiah's classic work: "The Lamentations of Jeremiah". Tradition from the old Jewish

Jeremiah — The Tired Teacher

Septuagint begins with these words: "And it came to pass that, after Israel was taken captive and Jerusalem was made desolate, Jeremiah sat weeping and lamented with this lamentation and said . . . " In an age when it is not manly to cry, Jeremiah would stick-out like a sour thumb, yet this is exactly what we need more today of. Men, who will weep over the ills of our country, cry over the injustice of society, and morn over the decline of the morals of our land. We need a Jeremiah to tell us the truth, show us the bitter end to our disobedience, and clearly show us our problems. We have too many preachers today simply giving the Good News, and we should, but we need to know the rest; the whole council of God, every oracle of the Almighty including the price for sin. A sick person needs their doctor to be honest about their aliment. A politician needs to be honest about the plagues affecting our land. The preacher must be straightforward in telling that judgment is coming for everyone that has forsaken the Lord and unless we repent and turn from our wicked ways we will face the wrath of God. Such messages will never make you popular. They will make you expendable to the mass media, the social elite, and the political correct. Even family and friends will turn on you, just as the family of Jesus and the citizen of Nazareth turned on Jesus; for 'a prophet will not be accepted in his own land' (Luke 4:24). This precept can be seen when you compare Jeremiah 1:1 with 11:21, 23.

What it was that made Jeremiah weep was the realization that the people of God were not going and would never repent despite his predictions and prophecy and preaching. The tears of lamentation were the result of a stiff-necked people stubbornly refusing to listen to their Lord. From the very beginning of Jeremiah's ministry he was warned of God that this would be the case, but he was commissioned anyway. It is my belief that Noah and Jeremiah had plenty to talk about in Abraham's Bosom, for like Jeremiah Noah, the preacher of righteousness (II Peter 2:5), prophesied for 120 years the impending doom of the world, yet in the end only seven people responded to his message; how many did Jeremiah have? Sin has a way of blinding the eyes of those that will not see (II Corinthians 4:4). As Noah couldn't stop the flood with his messages, neither could Jeremiah stop the invasion of Babylon with his sermons, and neither can I stop the flood of fire that will one day engulf this world (II Peter 3:16) with my sermons and messages. How often have I taken heart in the midst of my ministry from men like Jeremiah and Noah to keep on preaching despite the little response, to keep prophesying despite the harshness of the prediction, and to keep on proclaiming the truth about God despite the lack of listeners! Jeremiah was willing to expend all that the message would be delivered and so must we; nothing is too expendable for that end!

This kind of strain and stress does make its toll even on a mighty man of God. The verse that highlights the beginning of this devotional tells of a man who wants to quit and start an inn in the wilderness; of a preacher who wants to stop preaching to a stubborn congregation and get a secular job. Jeremiah wanted to leave the public-eye and go to a desert place for a rest. Many of us in the line of ministry like Jeremiah have forgotten the teaching of Jesus in Mark 6:31: " . . . Come ye yourselves apart into a desert place and rest a while . . . " We must learn to come apart before we come apart! We have never learned or forgotten that we have learned the importance of the precept to " . . . rest at noon . . . " (Song of Solomon 1:7) Someone has observed that "Rest is not a sedative for the sick, but a tonic for the strong!" Jeremiah needed an emancipation place, a transformation refuge. There seems to be a popular misconception today that God wants us to wear out for Him, tire out for the cause. Overwork is not God's idea for expendability. Jesus taught His disciples to rest, and God will provide even for His weeping prophets time to recover, recharge, and refresh themselves for the fight ahead. I love this story from Mrs. William Cowman's book, "Not Overwork But Overflow": "Tradition tells us that one day a hunter found the Apostle John seated on the ground playing with a tame quail. The hunter expressed his surprise that a man so earnest should be spending his time so profitlessly. John looked up at the hunter and said, 'Why is the bow on your shoulder unstrung?' To this the hunter replied, 'If kept always taut, it would lose its spring.' The kindly Apostle said with a smile, 'For the same reason I play with this bird!'"

I feel Jeremiah must have learned this lesson because he is remembered for his endurance and length of ministry despite the difficult years. Through three kingships Jeremiah persisted in his unpopular messages. Despite the continual efforts to silence him, Jeremiah kept on preaching the Words of God. It is not surprising that he often got discouraged, who of us hasn't, but he like Elijah was encouraged by God to keep on keeping on. Any preacher can tell stories of giving people godly advices only to witness their rejection of every Biblical concept. You watch people fall into terrible pits, pits that could have been avoided if only they had taken your advice, but you counsel on, preach on. Rejection and depression are no reasons to quit, stop preaching, and stop counseling. We are not sent to speak a soft message, an ear itching sermon, but a hard message to a hard-hearted world. Maybe we need the advice of Jesus about tomorrow (Matthew 6:34). Ours is not to bare the burdens of all our ministry, all our rejections, all our disappointments today, but just one at a time, one day at a time, one rejection at a time; so many of us try to carry more than one daily load. So maybe, you are the one that has been called to be the weeper of your family, of your church, or of your community. There seems to be always one that is called to weep **'the truth in tears'**! "Therefore thou shalt say this word unto them, let mine eyes run down with tears . . . " (Jeremiah 14:17)

37

ABNER—THE TREACHEROUS TRAITOR

II SAMUEL 3:27

And when Abner was returned to Hebron, Joab took him aside in the gate to speak with him quietly, and smote him there under the fifth rib, that he died, for the blood of Asahel his brother.

A LITTLE KNOWN CHARACTER OF the Bible, Abner was the son of King Saul's uncle. Because of his relationship to the king he rose quickly through the ranks until he became the captain of Saul's army. Because of his courage (I Samuel 26:15) and skill as a soldier, he maintained his influence over the army and the nation even after King Saul and most of his sons died at the Battle of Gilboa (I Samuel 31). I can't imagine that Abner wasn't at that battle too, but he survived to carry on the kingdom of Saul for a few more years. Abner is an example, in our ongoing study of 'being expendable', to the truth that no matter which side you choose, it will cost you dearly to 'switch sides' in the midst of the war; a lesson Abner would learn at the cost of his life!

Abner was a 'survivor' despite the very dangerous encounters he had all of his adult life. He no doubt was at the Battle of Elah when David slew Goliath. Even though he should have been one of the ones that should have stepped forward instead of a shepherd boy, he never lost his standing in the eyes of King Saul. Though David had become King Saul's armourbearer (I Samuel 16:21), Abner was ignorant of David's background (I Samuel

Abner—the Treacherous Traitor

17:55), but maintained his prominence by presenting David to the king after David's spectacular victory over the giant (I Samuel 17:57). Abner was an opportunist, and an opportunist runs the risk of being found out each time he makes a change from one side to another. Today we live in a world of opportunists; the philosophy of Abner is the accepted doctrine in the business world and I am afraid it has been accepted in the Church as well. Today people have come to love having one foot in the pew and the other in the aisle. If a trouble comes they are the first to the door, or if the wind changes they are the first to put their sail up to catch it. People like this never stay long enough to develop relationships, to put down roots, to become loyal; they are only loyal to themselves. People like Abner are always on the move because everything and everyone is expendable to their climbing the ladder they are on!

The next time we meet Abner in the Biblical text he is sleeping next to King Saul while David is creeping into their encampment to steal Saul's spear and water jug. (I Samuel 26:11) It is Abner that gets David's sharp rebuke for not protecting the king. (I Samuel 26:14) Abner saw his position, his office as self-promoting, self-serving. Often loyalty is not based on love or respect, but on what someone is able to get out of the job. David was really loyal to King Saul because David really loved the king (why else would David have spared Saul's life twice). The sad truth of King Saul and David's relationship was Saul drove away the one that really loved him and kept a man like Abner who was only in it for the power! Once again we have revealed the true character of men like Abner, men who are loyal for what they can get out of a relationship for themselves. Men like Abner are quick to discover how they can maneuver within the relationship for their own promotion. The tragedy is the Church has become a place for men like Abner; men who are found asleep when they should be on the alert. Paul warned the Church at Thessalonica of such men: "But ye, brethren, are not in darkness, that that day should overtake you as a thief. Ye are the children of light, and the children of the day: we are not of the night, nor of darkness. Therefore let us not sleep, as do others; but let us watch and be sober." (I Thessalonians 5:4–6) Abner proved in the end to be a child of the darkness and not a child of the day. I think the churchman Demas was such a man (II Timothy 4:10) as was the churchman Diotrephes (III John 9–11).

After the Battle of Gilboa, it was Abner that picked up the pieces and put the Kingdom of Saul back together by supporting and assisting Saul's son, Ishbosheth (II Samuel 2:8). Over the next two years Abner fought for

Ishbosheth to keep the house of Saul in power in Israel (II Samuel 2:10). In a play for the ultimate goal, the kingship itself, Abner sought to marry one of Saul's concubines and a falling out was the result between Ishbosheth and Abner. It was time for Abner to make his next move and that being an unauthorized alliance with David (II Samuel 3:21). Once again the political climate was changing and Abner realized that David would eventually be the next king of Israel and Ishbosheth's star was waning. In order for Abner to be on the winning side when the Civil war was over he had to jump ship, switch sides, turn coat, and be a traitor to his former boss. What Abner didn't count on was David's chief-of-staff, Joab. Abner had also forgotten the universal principle of " . . . reaping what you sow . . . " (Galatians 6:7–9) What goes around comes around for men like Abner, and the life of a traitor is a life in which pay back is often seen. Sooner or later men like Abner will run into men like Abner, and Joab was such a man. Little did Abner realize the day he lift the house of David with a signed agreement for his position in David's government that this would be his last day on earth: " . . . **pride does go before a fall . . .** " (Proverbs 16:18)

At the Battle of the Pool of Gibeon, Abner had killed Joab's brother Asahel (II Samuel 2:23). Joab and his other brother Abishai had tracked Abner after the killing but were unable to bring him to a fight. Years had passed but the anger and the desire for revenge hadn't until the peace conference at Hebron. Tricking Abner into returning under a flag of truce, Joab murdered Abner by killing him the same way Asahel had been killed (compare II Samuel 2:23 and II Samuel 3:27). The traitor had been betrayed. I believe Abner had let his guard down in the pride of his greatest accomplishment, his greatest switch. The one who had always taken pride in coming down on the right side, the winning side had lost and in turn had lost his life. The warning in the story of Abner is very clear to me: you can't play both sides against the other forever without getting caught! A time will come when you think you have pulled off the greatest double cross, a double switch only to find out that it is you that has been double crossed. Like Abner, you too will not see the knife until it is too late; until the knife of treason is unleashed. I find it interesting that one of the characteristics of the last days according to the Apostle Paul will be the abundance of " . . . traitors . . . " (II Timothy 3:4)

So we see again another illustration to Jesus' classic rebuke of Peter in the Garden of Gethsemane when He said: "Put up again thy sword into its place; for all that take the sword shall perish with the sword." (Matthew

27:52) John's Revelation verifies this concept with these words: "He that leadeth into captivity shall go into captivity; he that killeth with the sword must be killed with the sword." (Revelation 13:10) Is not this the story of Abner and so many more in the Bible? I have always loved the story of Adonibezek (Judges 1:4–7), the king that use to cut the toes and fingers off rulers he had captured; who in the end has his toes and fingers removed. People will face the same end as seen in the end of those that they have betrayed: sin for sin, 'eye for an eye' (Deuteronomy 19:21). Remember, the Christ-like life has so many more rewards!

38

METHUSELAH—THE PROPHETIC PATRIARCH

GENESIS 5:27

And all the days of Methuselah were nine hundred sixty and nine years; and he died.

As with Jonah 1:17, Genesis 5:27 has long been a focal point of critics of the Bible that believe the Scriptures only contain fairy tales, legends, and myths. Surely, no man could be swallowed by a fish and live, and surely, no man could live 969 years? It is upon this last story about the times of Methuselah that I would like to develop this 'expendable' devotional.

This strange but true story does contain some interesting principles revealed in the Word of God. Let me state right up front that even those who believe in the literal interpretation of the Bible there is a diversity of opinions on the Methuselah numbers and meaning, as it should be. It was the Apostle Peter that gave us this precept: "Knowing this first that no prophecy of scripture is of any private interpretation." (II Peter 1:20) As we will see, I believe Genesis 5:27 is a prophetic verse and we need to be careful in being too dogmatic about our interpretation; which leads us to a second important precept in Biblical interpretation: "Let every man be fully persuaded in his own mind." (Romans 14:5) Paul instructs us that we all have the right to believe what we believe, but we can't debate or discuss any interpretation dogmatically, feeling we and we alone have the answer. So

Methuselah—The Prophetic Patriarch

get out your commentaries, get out your concordance, get out your lexicon and let us study together the man that lived 969 years, and even after all that time was expendable to God, but on the day of his death; at the moment of his departure from this world, the world changed forever. As for me, I have come to this interpretation about the life and times of Methuselah.

Methuselah was the son of a very famous father, Enoch; of that we can all agree (Genesis 5:21). The first thing we can note from scripture is that something extraordinary happened to Enoch at the birth of Methuselah: "And Enoch walked with God AFTER (my capitals) he begat Methuselah." (Genesis 5:22) This indicates to me that before Methuselah's birth Enoch wasn't a God fearing man, didn't believe in, or walk in the ways of the Almighty. However, after Methuselah's birth Enoch walked with God for the next three hundred years? Enoch was a faithful follower to an exceptional end: "And Enoch walked with God and he was not for God took him." (Genesis 5:24) Paul gives us a better interpretation of exactly what happened in Hebrews 11:5-6: **"By faith Enoch was translated that he should not see death; and was not found, because God had translated him: for before his translation he had this testimony, that he pleased God. But without faith it is impossible to please Him: for he that cometh to God must believe that He is, and that He is a rewarder of them that diligently seek Him."**

What was it that happened at Methuselah's birth that turned his father around; brought his father into a relationship with God that lasted for as long as it did and resulted in Enoch's rapture? The Bible doesn't exactly tell us, but I believe by piecing these scriptures together we can come up with a logical and spiritual answer. First, we are told in Jude 14 that Enoch was a prophet. Second, many times in the Bible the birth of a child was used by God to reveal, or predict a future event. Consider the birth of the Hebrew prophet Hosea's three kids (Hosea 1:4-9), or the birth of Isaiah's children (Isaiah 8). I have come to believe it was at the naming of Enoch's son that God revealed to his prophet something that changed everything. If these conclusions are right then it all falls on the meaning of the name "Methuselah"? Now we come to our first controversy. There are some that simply believe the name Methuselah means 'man of the dart', but others believe it means: "he dies, and it is sent", a clear reference to those who believe in the coming of the universal flood of judgment. According to Jeremiah 28:9 and Deuteronomy 18:22, the test of a prophet is if his or her prophecy comes true?

At Methuselah's death did a flood come upon the earth? How can we tell? According to Genesis 5:27 Methuselah died in the 969th year of his life, and according to Genesis 7:11, in the 600th year of Noah's life, the flood arrived. If you graphed the years given in Genesis five on a time chart as I have done, and take into account the overlapping years of the lives of these antediluvian patriarchs you will find as I did that the 969th year of Methuselah and the 600th year of Noah are the same year from Adam: the year 1656! I believe the reason that Enoch changed his faith was the prophecy about the impending doom God had put on the earth. Long before God told Noah, he told Enoch. I believe Enoch was not willing to test the Word of God so he turned to God, but what of Methuselah? We know he wasn't on the ark, so did he die in the flood?

I have come to believe in something quite bold. I am convinced the names in Genesis 5 are the names of the righteous line (Genesis 4:26). You can't tell me if Noah told his family that Enoch didn't tell his family! I believe in the method of Biblical interpretation that takes something literally unless the text suggests otherwise (check John 2:18-21). So I read this literally: **"In the six hundredth year of Noah's life, on the seventeenth day of the second month-on that day all the springs of the great deep burst forth, and the floodgates of the heavens were opened."** (Genesis 7:11 NIV) I believe that the moment earth's longest living senior citizen took his last breath and died of natural causes (age) it began to rain for the very first time upon the earth (Genesis 2:5-6). I do not believe that Methuselah died in the flood judgment because he was of the godly, royal, and Messianic lines (Luke 3:37). Through faith, not hereditary, Methuselah was saved from the divine judgment of God.

So what should this tell us about God and His prophesies? God's prophecies should be taken seriously. Like Methuselah we live in an age of impending doom, a global judgment! Mankind has been predicting the end of the world for most of history; every generation has a prophet or two that sets a date, but all have been proven a false prophet. Man's predictions will fail, but God's have never failed. How did God know on the day of Methuselah's death the rains would come, for the same reason He knows when His Son will return (Matthew 24:36); the all-knowing God has foresight, foreknowledge! I believe like with that time this time will see those die before the time and some like Enoch will be raptured before the time (I Thessalonians 4:16-17), but many will die in the judgment (see the Revelation). Whichever case we need to get ready, for unlike Methuselah's time God has given the world more time to repent (969 years verses 2020 years at the time of this writing)! We must heed and hear the words of Peter in his second epistle (II Peter 3:3–7). The Lord will sacrifice His creation; the world is expendable!

Nobody living has or will have 969 years to ponder and plan for the end, and as sure as the sun came up in the east and will set in the west each day brings us closer to that ultimate day of judgment. Just as the dawn came to Methuselah's last day, I wonder if he was thinking of what his name ment, and if this was not the day. Paul tells us all: "**. . . now is the accepted time; behold, now is the day of salvation.**" II Corinthians 6:2)

39

MATTHEW—THE ACCOUNTANT APOSTLE

LUKE 5:27-28

And after these things He went forth, and saw a publican, named Levi, sitting at the receipt of custom: and He said unto him, Follow me. And he left all, rose up, and followed him.

FROM THIS BRIEF ENCOUNTER LEVI, also called Matthew (Matthew 9:9) became a disciple of the Lord Jesus Christ. For me, the expendable doctrine of the verse printed above is "he left all"! The other thing that stands out to me in the life of Levi is how often his profession is mentioned in relationship to his names. As Matthew himself lists the twelve apostles he writes: "*... Matthew the publican ...* " (Matthew 10:3) He doesn't write "Peter the fisherman", nor does he mention the other disciples in this way. Perhaps, Levi never wanted to forget where he came from and what he had to leave behind to be a disciple of Jesus. Whether we like it or not our past does come with us not matter where we come from, what we were, or when we were called. It isn't the Lord cares, for He calls those He wants, but people care and they will hold our past over our heads to the end. Expendable is part of the price one pays for following Christ; for some it is their possessions, others their position, and still others their place in society!

Long after Levi followed Jesus, the Christ was preaching when He made this statement: **"That the publicans and the harlots go into the kingdom of God before you!"** (Matthew 21:31) The 'you' were the Pharisees, but the 'publicans' were men like Matthew. At that time in Palestine there were two kinds of publicans (tax collectors or tax accountants). There were those who went from house to house collecting tribute for the Roman occupiers. Then there were those who were custom-house officials collecting taxes from the commerce of a particular area, like around the Sea of Galilee. Matthew seemed to have been of this later group (Luke 5:27). If these men were known for collecting what was due then they probably wouldn't have been so looked down upon, but they often collected more; lining their pockets in the process. The Romans didn't care as long as they got what they wanted. Remember the other famous publican in the Gospels, Zacchaeus. He seemed to be of the first group of tax collectors, for if you recall when he finally met Jesus and was converted that he promised to give back with interest the money he had stolen (Luke 19:8). Most publicans were Jewish, hired by the Romans, and so they were seen as traitors to their own people. Today, Levi would have been a bookkeeper for the Mafia. I often wonder after Matthew joined the disciple band if there were not some interesting conversation between him and men like James and John, Peter and Andrew and the taxes Matthew collecting from their fishing businesses?

Matthew was a convert from a contemptible profession, but Levi was not the only one. Rahab was a harlot and was converted and would eventually be a part of the Messianic line (Matthew 1:5) and would be numbered in the line of the most faithful (Hebrews 11:31). John Newton was a slave merchant, and he too got saved to give us one of the Church's most beloved hymns: "Amazing Grace"! I have a dear friend who is a converted bartender! Willy Mullen, the famous Irish preacher and pastor was a converted thief. Today my dear reader you might be caught up in a questionable profession and you are thinking that God has no interest in you, but He does! He found Matthew; He found Zacchaeus, and he found the adulterer at the well (John 4). You are just what He is looking for, but what we must remember is that when each heard the call 'they left all'! We have some today saying you can stay in your ungodly profession that it doesn't make any difference that you still tend bar, drive a beer truck, sell dope on the corner. Every story in the Bible like Levi's came out, walked away, and left all. Sometimes some old professions have to be seen as expendable when Jesus calls. If feel that there are just some professions Christians shouldn't be found: a Christian pimp, a Christian drug dealer, a Christian liquor salesman, or a Christian card dealer at the local casino!

Expendable

From a contemptible profession to a converted publican to a celebration party: "And Levi made him a great feast in house own house and there was a great company of publicans and of others that sat down with them." (Luke 5:29) Not only was there a party in heaven (Luke 15:10), but there was a party on earth. Levi wanted his old friends to know what had happened to him and he wanted them to meet Jesus. Is not this exactly what the Philippian jailer did after his famous conversion? (Acts 16:34) As we whoop-it-up we ought to witness. What is wrong with inviting all your old friends over, your old co-workers over, your old neighbors over for a conversion party? We forget to tell new converts this admonition from Jesus: "Whosoever therefore shall confess me before men, him will I confess also before my Father which is in heaven. But whosoever shall deny me before men, him will I deny before my father which is in heaven." (Matthew 10:32-33) Matthew is the only Gospel writer that prints that statement of Jesus; did he learn it following his conversion? I have met many over the years who we might call 'secret disciples'. I do believe there are such converts, men like Joseph of Arimathaea and Nicodemus (John 19:38), but sooner or later you must come out. It is tragic that more homosexuals are coming out of the closet than Christians! Granted, your new life in Christ might cost you some old friendships, but such friendships are expendable.

Nothing more is written in the Gospels and the Acts about the life of Matthew except in those situations and circumstances when the apostles are mentioned. But we have a whole lot more written by Levi. The book keeper changed professions and became a famous book writer. Instead of a how-to-do-it book titled: "Your Taxes and You", Levi wrote the bestseller: "The Gospel of Matthew" on the Life of the Christ. Jesus saw great potential in the tax collector and commissioned him to write a biography of the Him from the standpoint of Jewish history. Matthew's Gospel makes it clear through Hebrew prophecy that Jesus of Nazareth is the Messianic Messiah. You might never write a bestseller telling of your meeting Jesus, but our lives ought to be an open book to what Jesus did to us, for us, and in us. Paul highlights and underlines this precept in his epistle to the Church at Corinth: "Ye are our epistle written in our hearts known and read of all men. For as much as ye are manifestly declared to be the epistle of Christ ministered by us written not with ink, but with the Spirit of the Living God, not in tables of stone, but in fleshly tables of the heart." (II Corinthians 3:2-3) How is your book being read?

Levi took seriously Jesus' admonition: **"So likewise, whosoever he be of you that forsaketh not all that he hath, he cannot be my disciple."** (Luke 14:33) Unlike the rich young ruler, Matthew was willing to give up his possessions, his place, and his position to the cause of Christ. He like the others 'forsook all" (Luke 5:11) to follow the Christ. This concept is also lacking in our modern Christianity. Granted, our salvation costs us nothing, but our service to the King costs everything. Levi was willing to make that sacrifice, but are we? And Matthew was willing to make the ultimate sacrifice: " . . . and his own life also, he cannot be my disciple." (Luke 14:26) Levi's living was expendable. Levi's livelihood was expendable, and Levi's life was expendable! (Foxe's martyrs book)

40

ABISHAI—THE COOPERATIVE COMMANDER

I CHRONICLES 18:12

Moreover Abishai the son of Zeruiah slew of the Edomites in the Valley of Salt eighteen thousand.

WHEN DAVID NUMBERED HIS 'MIGHTY men', (I Chronicles 11:10) Abishai was fifth on that impressive list of warriors. His citation for bravery reads like this: **"And Abishai the brother of Joab, he was chief of the three: for lifting up his spear against three hundred, he slew them, and had a name among the three."** (I Chronicles 11:20 and II Samuel 23:18-19) What I find as interesting in this record of bravery that David leaves out the fact that Abishai singlehandedly killed a giant by the name of Ishbibenob, and in the process also saved David's life: **"And Ishbibenob, which was one of the sons of the giant, the weight of whose spear weighted three hundred shekels of brass in weight, he being girded with a new sword, thought to have slain David. But Abishai, the son of Zeruiah, succoured him, and smote the Philistine and killed him."** (II Samuel 21:16-17) As amazing as that seems, David's mind drifted back to a battle in which Abishai stood in the gap and killed 300 soldiers, not one giant soldier, even if that death resulted in saving the king's life! Could that stand and memorable act of courage have taken place in a war against of Edom and its most famous Battle in the Valley of Salt?

Abishai—The Cooperative Commander

Abishai was the second of three sons born to David's sister, Zeruiah (I Chronicles 2:15-16). All of Zeruiah's boys would eventually become part of David's grand army, and all of them would excel in daring and boldness and be numbered among David's elite, his "mighty men"! Joab, the oldest, would become chief of staff and run David's army (I Chronicles 11:6), and Asahel, the youngest, would give his life in pursuit of the mighty warrior Abner (II Samuel 2:18-23-expendable), but Abishai was the man, the cousin, the soldier that was always there at David's side when he needed someone! In the early days when David was still being hunted down by King Saul's forces, it was Abishai who went with David one night into the camp of the enemy and pulled off a daring raid to prove to King Saul that David's was no threat to him (I Samuel 26:6-9). Later, during the rebellion of Absalom, it was Abishai who came to David's defense in David's ignoble retreat from Jerusalem (II Samuel 16:9), and it was Abishai who commanded a third of David's army in the Battle of the Ephraim Woods that won the kingdom back for David (II Samuel 18:2). He was also there at the First Battle of Gob to save David's life from a giant (II Samuel 21:15-18) as we have mentioned before. Seemingly, at least in David's eyes, his crowning achievement on the battlefield and in the service of his king was his contribution in a war against Edom later in David's kingship. Was it here that Abishai lifted up his spear against 300 and won? No doubt many soldiers took part in the Battle of the Valley of Salt, but David mentions Abishai as being primarily responsible for the ultimate destruction of the Edomite army and the death of 18,000 warriors, why? If David would have given out medals, like The Congressional Medal of Honor (America's highest medal for bravery), I believe he would have given it to Abishai after this famous battle: " . . . . **for gallantry above and beyond the call of duty**"!

What is most interesting to me about this battle is the fact that it is mentioned in three Biblical places, and in each case a different person is given credit for the victory: Abishai in I Chronicles 18:12, Joab in Psalm 60, and David in II Samuel 8:13-14. One of the great abilities of talented military captains is the skill of leading men in a cooperative endeavor. Read carefully how David's three mightiest men, Adino, Eleazar, and Shammah, cooperated to get a cup of cold water from the well at the gate of Bethlehem (II Samuel 23:13-17)! There are those that interpreted this story as not being David's first three, but David's second three, Abishai, Benaiah, and Asahel (II Samuel 23:18-24)? Whichever the case, it was David that taught his soldier's team work. Team work wins battles that individuals can't win on their own. Like in basketball, five average players can win against a superstar any time, even if you are LeBron James! I like the definition of George M. Verity on cooperation: **"Cooperation is really spelled with two letters-WE!"** I have come to believe that Abishai was a 'we-person'. Whenever you read about Abishai in the Bible it is Abishai and somebody else: like his brother Joab or his king David. Abishai was a team player and he didn't care if he got the glory or not or where he played; he was ready and willing to do whatever it took for the team to win. Whether with others or alone it was always 'we' not 'me' when it came to the warrior Abishai!

There seems to be a lot of Christians today working for the Lord rather than working with the Lord. Paul taught the Church: "For we are labourers together with the Lord" (I Corinthians 3:9); take time this week to read the context of that precept (I Corinthians 3:4–8 and I Corinthians 12:12–27). Harry C. Mabry tells a fable that illustrates wonderfully this great truth about spiritual warfare: "A man had just arrived in Heaven, and told Saint Peter how grateful he was to be in such a glorious place, and asked Saint Peter to give him one glimpse into Hades in order that he might appreciate his good fortune even more. This Saint Peter did. In Hades, he saw a long table extending as far as the eye could see laden down with the most delicious foods, but everybody was staring to death. When asked for an explanation Saint Peter answered: 'Everybody is required to take food from the table only with four-foot long chopsticks. The chopsticks are too long to use for one's self, but in Hades nobody helps or cooperates. That is why they are all starving.' Quickly Saint Peter and the man returned to Heaven, and behold, the new arrival saw an identical table, laden with the same delicious food, but everyone around the heavenly table was happy and well-fed. Then the man asked Saint Peter, 'With what do they take food from the table?' And Saint Peter replied: 'Four-foot chopsticks!' At that the newest resident of Heaven asked: 'Then why are those in Hades starving while all those in Heaven are healthy and full?' Whereupon Saint Peter answered: **'In Heaven, we feed each other!'"**

Two of the verses that has help me the most in understanding the success of David and his mighty men are I Chronicles 11:9–10: **"So David waxed greater and greater: for the Lord of Hosts was with him. There also (including Abishai) are the chief of the mighty men whom David had, who strengthened themselves with him in his kingdom, and with all Israel, to make him king, according to the word of the Lord concerning Israel."** It wasn't just God, or just David, or just the mighty men. It was like Paul taught; it was a planting Paul, a watering Apollos, and the Lord that gives the increase! Whether the war of Edom or the battle we wage every day against the forces of sin, self, and Satan, cooperation is a source of wealth we have that should never be overlooked! Philippians 2:2-Fulfill ye my joy, that ye be likeminded, having the same love, being of one accord, of one mind. Selfishness (the idol of me) is expendable to those who want to win the game verses those who want the glory of winning the game!

41

REUBEN—THE BURDENSOME BOY

GENESIS 35:22

And it came to pass, when Israel dwelt in that land, that Reuben went and lay with Bilhah his father's concubine: and Israel heard of it. Now the sons of Jacob were twelve.

ONLY THOSE WHO HAVE A wayward son can possible understand what I am about to share in this 'expendable' article on the life and times of Reuben, the firstborn son of Jacob (Genesis 29:32). Recently, the Lord reminded me of this precept from the pen of Paul in which he wrote: **"Hath not the potter power over the clay, of the same lump to make one vessel unto honour, and another unto dishonor?"** (Romans 9:21) How can out of the same womb come an Esau and a Jacob; a Reuben and a Judah; and out of the same womb come a Scott and a Marnie (my children)? How can two children raised under the same roof, by the same rules, taken to the same church, and instructed in the same way turn out so different; only God can make from the same clay one an instrument to honorable things and the other an instrument to evil things, but why? Why is one child expendable to the nature of evil and wicked things?

What joy there was in the tents of Jacob when Leah gave birth to their first born son; a boy they called Reuben. When Reuben's birth came all the rights of being the first born son into a Jewish family, yet Reuben, like Esau, never received a single blessing. In a family where position of birth was everything, when it came to ultimate blessings, not one firstborn every attained to the goal: remember Isaac was Abraham's second son, Jacob was a second son, and Judah was the fourth son, the one that got the Messianic blessing. It was Joseph's second son Ephraim that got the Israelite blessing, and it was Amram's second son Moses that God called to be the redeemer of Israel. It was David's last son that attained to the throne of Judah. From these events we see that God is not dependent on the traditions of men, the birthright and blessing of the firstborn, but God looks at the heart of men. God choice is based on His purpose and plan, not the order one is born. We have seen before in this series of expendable devotions that faith is the key to reward, blessing (Hebrews 11:6). Like Reuben and many before and after him, some children turn out to be a burden not a blessing. I am afraid I know all too well the burden a dishonorable son can cause. Reuben was not the first or the last that brought disgrace and shame on the family, and if you have such a son, you too know of what I am writing!

In the study of Reuben's life I have come to the conclusion that Reuben is a perfect picture of the 'old man' nature inherited from father Adam (Romans 5:12). This is one of the aspects no parent can totally correct or improve on. Our DNA will produce certain qualities and characteristics, but the Adamic nature comes with each child (Psalm 51:5). Despite this there is hope that through instruction in righteousness and proper discipline and a good example that bent in our nature can be straightened out over time. Paul teaches that through grace and the work of the Holy Spirit we can " . . . put off concerning the former conversation (behavior) the old man which is corrupt according to the deceitful lusts." (Ephesians 4:22) Reuben never did get rid of that old man nature, and neither did my son. The stigma was there throughout their lives. For men like Reuben and Scott it is a lifelong struggle that always rears its ugly head. It appears from Scripture that Reuben never conquered it, and as for my son; I write this on the eve of his 40th birthday, but he is not here for six month ago he was taken by cancer. In the final six months of his life Scott sought forgiveness and his mother and I believe came back to a rightful relationship with his Maker, but most of his adult life was a Reuben life!

Reuben's signature sin is recorded in the verse I have printed for you above. The lust of the flesh eventually caught up to Reuben, and a sin " . . . not so much as named among the Gentiles, that one should have his father's wife . . . " (I Corinthians 5:1); a particular fornication most grievous. Do I believe that Reuben was a believer in the God of Abraham, Isaac, and

Jacob? Yes I do! But we should never forget that even men of faith can sin sins worse than the unbeliever. Sinning is still a part of the nature of man even after salvation (I John 1:8–10). Reuben's sin would haunt him for the rest of his life, and even the Bible would never let him forget (I Chronicles 5:1). And though my son's sin '... **that so easily beset...**' (Hebrews 12:1) him wasn't the same sin, it was a sin that hounded him to his last day, and though he has gone still horrifies his mother until her death just eight months ago, and I to this day. These might be unforgettable sins, but praise the Lord they are not unforgivable sins! Will I meet Reuben in Heaven; I believe so, just like I believe I will meet my son there!

Years after this one event in Reuben's life he was standing beside the deathbed of his father Jacob and hear this: **"Reuben thou art my first born my might and the beginning of my strength, the excellency of dignity and the excellency of power, unstable as water thou shalt not excel because thou wentest up to thy father's bed then defiledst thou it: he went up to my couch."** (Genesis 49:3–4) As with Jacob I am still having a hard time to forget what Scott did, but though I probably never well; through the Blood of Christ I believe the Father has. Reuben's curse seemingly was passed down to Reuben's descendants (Scott had no children). Even when the Chronicles were recorded we have this: "Now the sons of Reuben the first born of Israel for he was the first born but forasmuch as he defiled his father's bed his birthright was given unto the sons of Joseph and the genealogy is not to be reckoned after the birthright." (I Chronicles 5:1) Think with me of any famous Reubenites? Reuben's one act of lust (or was he trying to claim the birthright) marred his legacy and his family forever. How we need to remember the admonition of Paul when he wrote: **"Flee fornication. Every sin that a man doeth is without the body but he that committeth fornication sinneth against his own body."** (I Corinthians 6:18) Sins might not be held against generations, but sins will affect generation after generation by their implications!

Let us take seriously our part in the first role, or the first example of anything. Maybe, you like me are the first born son of a generation, or a family. With that position comes a responsibility to live a life exemplary; something I could never get through to my son, but something that I have understood all my life. Maybe, you are the first to begin a new work or a new ministry. The entire future of that work or ministry will depend on how you work and minister during your lifetime. By what you do and say, those who come after you will be affected either for good or ill. Will you pass on a blessing or a burden to those that follow you? Many leave a burden like Reuben, a burden that others will have to carry with them. I know I haven't answered my original question: why does God out of the same lump of clay create a vessel of honor and a vessel of dishonor? I have no answer because I still don't understand the mind of Christ in this. I still struggling even after 3 years wondering why God would take Scott so early in life; why was he the way he was and Marnie the way she is? To be the first to only blow it! To start the race only to fail it! To face the first temptation only to yield to it! But this I have come to understand that as I wait for God's revealing answer; that God's grace is sufficient. (II Corinthians 12:9)

42

DANIEL—THE SUPPLICATING STATEMAN

DANIEL 6:22

My God hath sent his angels, and hath shut the lion's mouths, that they have not hurt me: forasmuch as before him innocency was found in me; and also before thee, O king, have I done no hurt.

HAVE YOU IN YOUR STUDY of the Bible figured out yet why Satan wanted to get rid of the captive Daniel? I have come to believe it was for the same reason that Lucifer wanted to get rid of the patriarch Job! Both where men of prayer; compare Job 1:5, 21 and Daniel 6:10. If I have learned anything from my reading of the Bible it is the fact that the Devil hates men or women of prayer. Jesus was a man of prayer, and we all know how the Wicked One hounded and haunted Jesus to the Cross of Calvary, and that there is only one way to silence a man of prayer and that is to kill him! Remember that the Apostle Paul was a man of prayer and how many times did the Devil try to kill him? I have just finished a two year teaching through the Book of Job and I have become convinced that it exactly what Satan was after when he tried to get permission from the Almighty to kill Job (Job 2:4–6). I am also convinced that was the reason Satan was behind the plot to see that Daniel would be thrown into the den of lions. Lucifer was out to silence a prayer warrior, for with the Wicked One all such soldiers of supplication are expendable!

Daniel—The Supplicating Statesman

I believe most people who read the Book of Daniel miss the significance of the story of the lion's den because the book wasn't written in chronological order. I have become convinced in my study of this classic prophetic book that chapter six and chapter nine happened at the same time. Note carefully: "In the first year of Darius the son of Ahasuerus, of the seed of the Medes, which was made king over the realm of the Chaldeans; in the first year of his reign I Daniel understood by books the number of the years, whereof the Word of the Lord came to Jeremiah the prophet, that he would accomplish seventy years in the desolation of Jerusalem. And I set my face unto the Lord God to seek by prayer and supplication, with fasting, and sackcloth, and ashes: and I prayed unto the Lord, and made my confession, and said . . . " (Daniel 9:1-4) So what was Daniel doing praying three times a day (Daniel 6:10); what was the urgency that committed him to prayer despite the danger? I have come to believe that Daniel was praying the Jews back to Jerusalem! This was certainly something the Devil didn't want to happen. No Jews in the Promised Land, no Messiah would or could come! Satan had slipped into the void and was re-occupying the land with his own people; the way he did when Jacob took his family out of Canaan to Egypt. As Satan tried to block the Israelites back into the land in the days of Moses and Joshua, so he would try again to block the Jews from getting back into the land after the Babylonian Captivity. If he could succeed he could destroy the fulfillment of the birth of the Christ. Satan knew God's plan and he knew the importance of the land and the people of Israel in that plan. That is why the plot to kill Daniel was a diabolical plan to rid Israel of its number one supplicator (Daniel 6:4). The Devil has always known that " . . . the effectual fervent prayer of a righteous man availeth much . . . " (James 5:16 And Daniel was such a man.

The exploits of Daniel in intercessory prayer should teach us two things about prayer. One, that persistence in prayer should be a priority; no matter what the danger might be. "And he (Jesus) spake a parable unto them to this end that men ought always to pray and not to faint." (Luke 18:1) "Now when Daniel knew that the writing was signed he went into his house and his windows being open in his chamber towards Jerusalem, he kneeled upon his knees three times a day and prayed and gave thanks before the Lord as he did aforetime." (Daniel 6:10) What do you allow to interfere with your prayer time; whether private prayers or public prayers? Few Christians are left who have made prayer a priority; I will just remind you of the Wednesday Night Prayer Meeting as an example. Oh, there are a few who come regularly, but most allow anything else to stop them. Other meetings, a ball game, a night shopping, a party are all priorities now! Daniel was the type that would be at a prayer meeting no matter what, and so should we! It should also be true of our private prayer times. Most today give God their left-over time; time in which we have nothing better to do. Daniel gave God his "prime time" and he believed in the admonition from the pen of the Psalmist when he wrote: **"Evening, and morning, and at noon will I pray and cry aloud, and He shall hear my voice."** (Psalm 55:17) Maybe it is time we check just how persistent we are in our praying, supplicating, and interceding. Could this be the reason we are not surviving the lion den experiences of our life, or the reason the Church is in such trouble today? Let us never forget that the Bible likens the Devil to " . . . a roaring lion seeking who he may devour . . . " (I Peter 5:8), and the Wicked One has a huge appetite for people who pray; men like Daniel.

And two, protection is always provided for the prayer warrior no matter the day: even the day of the lion. In the story of Daniel chapter six, Daniel of course was caught (Daniel 6:11), charged (Daniel 6:13), and convicted (Daniel 6:16), but he was not afraid. How Daniel's enemies must have thought: "We have him now," and smiled as they watched Daniel descending into the dungeon of lions? Much like the enemies of Christ smiled as He was led off to Golgotha's hill, raised over Calvary's hill, and breathe His last breath on the Skull of a hill. Since the day of Abel, the wicked and the Wicked One have applauded while the righteous die believing their devilish schemes have succeeded, but they forget this one Scriptural precept: "No weapon that is formed against thee shall prosper . . . " (Isaiah 54:17) When prayer warriors like Daniel come into direct conflict with the enemies of God, God's integrity is at stake; His name is on the line, so He intervenes. The morning after being thrown into the lion's den Daniel tells Darius what happened: "My God sent His angel and He shut the mouths of the lions. They have not hurt me, because I was found innocent in His sight." (Daniel 6:22 NIV); just like God sent His angel to protect Peter from Herod (Acts 12); another great prayer warrior; just like God sent His angel to protect Hananiah, Azariah, and Michael from Nebuchadnezzar (Daniel 3), and so God will send His messenger to protect you. It was the Psalmist that also wrote: "The angel of the Lord encampeth round about them that fear Him and delivereth them." (Psalm 34:7) Daniel was just as safe in the lion's den as he was in his own bedroom; his prayer closet? Our place and position might change, but if you are one of God's children your protection

Daniel — the Supplicating Stateman

will never change. We may sleep, we may sleep with a lion as our pillow, but "He that keepeth Israel shall neither slumber nor sleep." (Psalm 121:4) A prayer warrior needs to be persistent in the belief that he will be protected.

What I believe we need to learn from the story of Daniel and the lion's den is that Satan might think the prayer warrior is expendable, but God doesn't! A prayer warrior like Daniel will be safe and secure to continue to pray even in a lion's den, or in a lion's mouth! What do you think Daniel was doing in the den? I have come to believe that he was supplicating, not for himself, but for his people and their return to Jerusalem! Is there something or someone you need to be praying for three times a day?

43

Jonah—The Reluctant Reverend

Jonah 1:17

Now the Lord had prepared a great fish to swallow up Jonah. And Jonah was in the belly of the fish three days and three nights.

The very mention of the Assyrians brought fear to the hearts of the men of Jonah's day. This people group from northern Iran was the scourge of the planet in Jonah's time, and though others like them would follow after them, they are still considered by those who study ancient history one of the worst groups ever to inhabit this planet. A ruthless, murderous, evil, wicked, and vile nation, they would through brute force and violence laid claim to the whole of the Middle East before their rampaging was over. No army, no nation, no people dare to oppose them at the height of their power, for their cruelty was unmatched in that day. If Assyria caused men to quake, Nineveh made men run in the opposite direction, but it was to this place the missionary, prophet, evangelist Jonah was sent. Nineveh was the capital of this rouge nation; where the worst of the worst lived. Located on the banks of the Tigris River, this ancient city was an impressive sight and site to those who got to travel to its fabled streets. Eighteen miles long and fourteen miles wide, this stronghold was surrounded by one hundred foot walls, and on these wall were 1500 towers! It was a rich city made wealthy by the plunder and booty stolen from every country in the Fertile Crest. Its fortress impregnable, its army invincible; it was undefeated by the time a lone Jewish preacher arrived at its front gate, for despite it ungodliness and wickedness God didn't think Nineveh was expendable, but what about His prophet? **"Now the Word of the Lord came unto Jonah the son of Amittai, saying, arise, go to Nineveh, that great city, and cry against it; for their wickedness is come up before me."** (Jonah 1:1-2)

As in the lives of people and nations there comes a time for divine judgment; a day to one and all! As with Babel (Genesis 11) and Sodom (Genesis 19) before her, God's hour glass of grace was running out for Nineveh. Nineveh only had a short time left to repent or feel the wrath of God's hand of judgment. God assigned His prophet Jonah to proclaim the message of impending doom, **"... but Jonah rose up to flee unto Tarshish from the presence of the Lord ..."** (Jonah 1:3) Tarshish was at the other end of the Mediterranean Sea, the furthest point in the then known world one could go in the opposite direction to Nineveh. God's man was running, fleeing, rebelling against his assignment and mission. Instead of an evangelistic crusade in Nineveh the reluctant reverend decided a Mediterranean cruise to Tarshish was more to his liking! How many times have we opted out for a vacation when the God Lord would have us do something in connection with our vocation? (Ephesians 4:1) Have you ever run from a difficult calling, a distasteful visit, or a dangerous assignment? I know that Jonah has gotten a lot of flak over the years from the commentators and preachers, but I wonder if we had been in his shoes if we wouldn't have come to the same conclusion: why should I spend my time evangelizing wicked people who will never repent in the end?

However God, instead of re-assigning the project to another evangelist, God goes after Jonah. Instead of writing off Jonah and letting him enjoy his holiday, God gives Jonah a bit of rope and then pulls him back. Even direct disobedience, stark rebellion doesn't change the eternal plans of God. People might try to alter God's divine will, but ultimately God's will is fulfilled. I think God even takes into account our side-steps, or detours into His purpose to teach us classic precepts like: "For the gifts and calling of God are without repentance." (Romans 11:29) The next time you hear someone say: "Let someone else do it!" You remind them of Jonah and Nineveh. Jonah was God's man for the mission, and Nineveh was Jonah's flock and calling. I have met so many believers in my travels running from their spiritual responsibilities with the attitude that if they don't do it God will call someone else to do it. I am convinced that is why a lot of things never get done; the person who was supposed to do it is on vacation, and

God is waiting their return. He will not assign someone else to your job! It is your business; your ministry, and ultimately only you can do it. You are not expendable in the service of the King!

How did God get the rebel back on track to Nineveh? In one of the most amazing stories of history, the Bible explains God's method of recalling and reassigning Jonah this way. Add to the verse I printed above to this line from the Book of Jonah: "... **and the Lord commanded the fish, and it vomited Jonah onto dry land ...** " (Jonah 2:10) Many don't believe this story, but I learned at a very early age it only takes one story of the Bible to be disbelieved and soon the whole book is questioned. I can't explain it, but I believe Jonah was swallowed by a great fish; was in its belly for three full days and nights travelling back towards land and at the end of that trip the fish vomited the reluctant reverend onto dry land. It was God's fish dealing with God's man in God's way. Those who question the ways of God or His methods will probably within their lifetime experience a Jonah adventure. The fish tale was simply God's method of bringing his wandering messenger back to his assignment.

Why Jonah was so reluctant to go to Nineveh is never mentioned in the narration? Was he simply afraid of the Ninevehites? Was he anger at the way the Assyrians had treated his people when they invaded Israel? Was he apathetic toward the heathens; only concerned with God's chosen people? Who really knows but Jonah and God? God must have concluded that these facts were not necessary to the telling of the story and the importance of what this mission was all about. For me, what is important is the truth that God always gives His servants a second chance: **"And the Word of the Lord came unto Jonah the second time saying ..."** (Jonah 3:1) Don't let the Devil convince you that you are no longer needed by God and no longer necessary; that He has put you on a shelf! Praise the Lord for the God of the second chance; for the grace and mercy of God that will forgive a reluctant reverend and put him back into Christ's service. Over the years this has brought me back from many a mishap in the ministry. I found this saying a few years back that has encouraged me: **"Out of the will of God there can be no success; in the will of God there can be no failure!"** For we read that "... Jonah obeyed the Word of the Lord and went to Nineveh ... On the first day, Jonah started into the city. He proclaimed: Forty more days and Nineveh will be overthrown ... The Ninevehites believed God. They declared a fast, and all of them, from the greatest to the least, put on sackcloth ... When God saw what they did and how they turned from their wicked ways, he had compassion and did not bring upon them the destruction He had threatened." (Jonah 3:3, 4, 5, 10 NIV) The result of Jonah's messages was the greatest recorded revival in ancient times. Who wouldn't want to be a part of such a spiritual awakening, an evangelistic miracle? **Never forget when God calls He has a wonderful event planned!**

44

Elisha—The Conquering Corpse

II Kings 13:21

And it came to pass, as they were burying a man, that, behold, they spied a band of men; and they cast the man into the sepulchre of Elisha: and when the man was let down, and touched the bones of Elisha, he revived, and stood up on his feet.

ONE OF THE MOST DIFFICULT and interesting teaching of our Lord and Saviour Jesus Christ was the principle He gave His disciples in this instruction: **"He that findeth his life shall lose it, and he that looseth his life for my sake shall find it."** (Matthew 10:39) Just before His own death Jesus explained this precept in light of his own life with these words: **"Verily, verily, I say unto you, except a corn of wheat fall into the ground and die, it abideth alone, but if it die, it bringeth forth much fruit. He that loveth his life shall lose it, and he that hateth his life in this world shall keep it unto life eternal."** (John 12:24-25) I believe we have in the Scripture printed above an illustration of this very concept, and the principle that even's God's greatest prophets were expendable, but even when they die they still have great power. Jesus would also teach: " . . . **I am the resurrection, and the life: he that believeth in me, though he were dead, yet shall he live: and whosoever liveth and believeth in me shall never die. Believeth thou this?"** (John 11:25-26) Have you ever considered the death of Elisha in light of these teaching of our Lord?

Elisha—the Conquering Corpse

Elisha, the great prophet and companion of Elijah had died as all great men and women do: "Now Elisha was fallen sick of his sickness, whereof he died!" (II Kings 13:14) Remember, God has determined how each of us will die (Revelation 1:18), not the Devil, or disease, or disaster! It was 'his sickness' by which he died. The man of God that had held Israel together spiritually for many years with his miracles and messages had finally yielded to the end of all of us, death: "And it is appointed unto them once to die . . ." (Hebrews 9:27) Yet this man had asked and received at the departure of his master Elijah " . . . a double portion . . . " (II Kings 2:9–14 of Elijah's spirit. Therefore, Elisha's life became a textbook on the power of God on a man's life, through a man's life, and in a man's life. I would remind you of this in this short outline and summary of Elisha's life:

1. Elisha destined for Power-I Kings 19:16: Elisha's called by Elijah to be his servant and after his departure his heir-apparent.
2. Elisha deserving of Power-I Kings 19:20: Elisha was willing to leave his family and their farm for the wandering life of a prophet.
3. Elisha disciple to Power-I Kings 19:21: Elisha followed Elijah wherever he went and learned the trade of the prophet of God.
4. Elisha determined for Power-II Kings 2:2: Elisha was determined not to leave his master's side until they were separated by Elijah's departure.
5. Elisha desirous for Power-II Kings 2:9: Elisha asked from his master one final thing and that being a 'double portion' of his Spirit.
6. Elisha demonstrates the Power-II Kings 2:14: Elisha performs the same miracle of Elijah and that was the parting of the Jordan River.
7. Elisha deathly Power-II Kings 13:21: Elisha's bone, even in the grave, still contained enough power to resurrect.

Elisha's life and death was nothing short of a channel for the power of God to flow through. The miracles of Elisha were shown to be equal to the power demonstrated to Moses, Elijah, and Jesus Himself. There were no times in history where such a pattern of miraculous signs were given to the world. Remember with me Elisha's miracles and the miracles of the Big Three. Elisha showed God's power over nature with the parting of the Jordan (II Kings 2:12–14), the purifying of the water (II Kings 2:19–22), and the puddles of water to quench the thirst of a dying army (II Kings

Expendable

3:1–22). I think of Elijah's parting, Jesus on the Sea of Galilee, and Moses at the Red Sea. Elisha showed God's power over the animal kingdom in his judgment on the irreverent children (II Kings 2:23–25). Like Jesus Elisha multiplied food (II Kings 4:42–44), raised the dead (II Kings 4:8–37), healed the leper (II Kings 5:1–19), and made the blind to see again (II Kings 6:8–23). God's power through Elisha included the multiplication of oil (II Kings 4:1–7-Jesus multiplied food), cleansing of poisonous food (II Kings 4:38–41-Moses poisonous snakes bites cured), and to make ax head's swim (II Kings 6:1–7-Jesus walked on water). In all these miracles none for me compares to the miracle that took place after Elisha's death. In the strangest story from Elisha's amazing feats empowered by the Almighty, the one of the resurrected corpse is for me the most fascinating: expendable but not eliminated!

How long Elisha had been buried we don't know, but I believe by the time the newly dead man was thrown into Elisha's sepulchre all that was left were Elisha's died up bones, but there was still power in those bones; leftover power from the days of Elisha's 'double spirit' gift from God. I believe the spirit of Elisha was long gone given the teaching of Ecclesiastes 12:7: "Then shall the dust return to the earth as it was: and the spirit shall return unto God who gave it." But the power remained! God's power was still evident in the skeleton of Elisha. Just like God's presence was still present in the face of Moses after their encounter on top of the Mount Sinai (Exodus 34:29–35). We often forget that the death of one of God's saints in not an end but a glorious continuation. The Psalmist penned these lovely words in relationship to this concept: "Surely, he shall not be moved forever, the righteous shall be in everlasting remembrance." (Psalm 112:6) There ought to be a wondrous posthumous influence of all saints. I like what Paul wrote about Abel (a fellow we have already looked at in our examination of God's expendables) after his death: "By faith Abel offered unto God a more excellent sacrifice than Cain, by which he obtained witness that he was righteous, God testifying of his gifts and by it be being dead yet speaketh." (Hebrews 11:4) Elisha being dead yet speaketh of the power of God in the resurrection of the unnamed and unknown man!

When you or I are layed in the ground, or scattered above ground will there be any evidence that we actually lived? I have become convinced that Jesus was speaking of this doctrine to His disciples when he admonished them with these words: "Ye have not chosen me, but I have chosen you, and ordained you, that ye should go and bring forth fruit, and that your fruit should remain . . . " (John 15:16) Will you leave any leftover sign that God's power was in and on your life; that He worked through your life? So many people have only a tombstone, a marker to verify their presence in this old world. What a tragedy! What a waste! Have you as of yet died to this world and the things of this world for the world to come? We need to turn to the only life (John 14:6) that will give us any hope of leaving something behind to affect someone left behind our wake. Only in that life, like Elisha's life, will we have the power to live long after death. Expendable doesn't mean just because you die that God isn't through with you! (I Thessalonians 4:16–17)

45

Gideon—The Fleece Fighter

Judges 6:38

And it was so: for he (Gideon) rose up early on the morrow, and thrust the fleece together, and wringing the dew out of the fleece, a bowl full of water.

Are you a believer in putting out a 'fleece' when you don't really know what to do?

I have been listening to the spiritual debate that has been raging for centuries over the spiritual significance of seeking a sign verses simply trusting God's Word. The super pious will argue that any fleece is a sign of spiritual weakness in faith; a spiritual immaturity of the individual. Yet when one takes a serious study of the Bible you will find no direct commandment against the 'fleece', or the practice of asking God for a sign to strengthen your faith. So what then is the doctrine of the 'fleece'? I have come to believe the Scriptures teach us that faith is not expendable when a fleece is requested!

Gideon was a young man from Ophrah when he was called of the Lord to deliver His people from the servitude of the Midianites. If one reads carefully the story of Gideon (Judges 6–9), from the very first encounter with 'the angel of God' (Jesus?), Gideon was a believer that needed reassurance: **"And the Lord said unto him, Surely I will be with thee, and thou shalt smite the Midianites as one man. And he said unto him, if now I**

have found grace in thy sight, then shew me a sign that thou talkest with me." (Judges 6:16–17) Gideon was simple asking: "Is it really you Lord?" Before we are too hard on Gideon ask yourself what you would have done? Oh, we boldly say we would never doubt, but don't get to critical until you have a direct visitation from 'the angel of the Lord', or the Lord Himself!

What happened next is carefully recorded by Herbert Lockyer in his classic book of "All the Men of the Bible": "The same night of the angelic appearance, God commanded Gideon to take a young bullock from his father's flock and, destroying his altar to Baal, to build another altar and offer a sacrifice upon it to Him. At night, Gideon carried out the task. In the morning, when Joash (Gideon's father) came to know of the daring action of his son against this idolatrous worship, in a cunning way he told those who sought the life of his son Gideon for his destruction of the Baal altar, to let Baal plead himself. It was on this day that Joash changed his son's name from Gideon to Jerubbaal, the latter name meaning 'the antagonist of Baal'. Gideon, true to his name which signifies 'the hewer', was not afraid to stand almost alone among a wicked and apostate people as a true worshiper of Jehovah." There are some in the commentaries who write that his raid at night was a sign of a coward, not a hero; a weakness not a bravery, but we should first make note that again God never rebuked Gideon for his night action, just like he was never rebuked in the first encounter when Gideon asked for a sign. I believe a pattern is developing that will help answer the question that introduces this devotional! It is then not surprising that if Gideon asked for a sign from 'the angel of the Lord' that he would ask for another sign, actually a double sign when the Lord finally revealed to Gideon his primary mission: the destruction of the Midianites army in Jezreel.

The Midianites and some allies of this roaming, Bedouin people had encamped in the valley of Jezreel in central Canaan. Once located the Spirit of the Lord came upon Gideon to call Israel to battle against this destructive plague pillaging the land. As men began to gather to Gideon's banner, Gideon asked for his now famous signs, or as some will say his infamous, double, divine sign. (Judges 6:36–40) Where some see doubt, I actually see trust. I have come to believe that Gideon was a man of the soil, but also a man of the Scriptures. Could Gideon have been trusting in some divine precepts that would only be written later by the prophets? What about this future truth: "By His knowledge the depths are broken up, and the clouds drop down the dew!" (Proverbs 3:20) Did Gideon believe that God was in control of the dew? The prophet Hosea would write hundreds of years later:

"I will be as the dew unto Israel . . . " (Hosea 14:5) God saw God in the dew. The morning dew was a symbol of the presence of Jehovah to men like Gideon. A pure, natural event was turned into a supernatural occurrence when the dew only fell as Gideon requested. For me, Gideon's request of God was similar to Hezekiah's request of God: "It is a light thing for the shadow to go down ten degrees: nay, but let the shadow return backwards ten degrees." (II Kings 20:10) An easy thing just to let the dew fall or not to fall, but to fall on a single fleece, or fall all around a single fleece now that is something that only God can do. To let a clock go forward is natural; to turn a clock back is supernatural. Difficult for man to do let alone explain, yet the man of faith always asks His God for the tough signs. Was this any more difficult than for Joshua to ask God for the sun and the moon to stand still? There is no doubt in the mind of Paul that Gideon was a man of faith, for he would pen to the Hebrews: "And what shall I say more? For time would fail me to tell of Gideon . . . " (Hebrews 11:32)

I like what Mrs. Charles Cowman recorded in her famous devotional book "Streams in the Desert" about faith: "There are degrees to faith. At one stage of Christian experience we cannot believe unless we have some sign of some great manifestation of feeling. We feel our fleece, like Gideon, and if it is wet we are willing to trust God. This may be true faith, but it is imperfect. It always looks for feeling or some token besides the Word of God. It marks quite an advance in faith when we trust God without feeling. It is blessed to believe without having emotion. There is a third stage of faith which even transcends that of Gideon and his fleece. The first phase of faith believers when there are favorable emotions, the second believes when there is the absence of feeling, but the third form of faith believes God and His Word when circumstances, emotions, appearances, people, and human reason all urge to the contrary. Paul exercised this faith in Acts 27:20, 25: 'And when neither sun nor stars in many days appeared, and no small tempest lay unto us, all hope that we should be saved was taken away . . . notwithstanding all this Paul said, Wherefore, sirs, be of good cheer; for I believe God, that it shall be even as it was told me." May God give us faith to fully trust His Word through everything else witness the other way. I am not saying that 'fleece faith' is great faith, like the centurion's faith (Matthew 8:5–10); I am simply saying it is faith.

Continue looking through the story you will find that Gideon faith was consistent, it seemed never to grow. Even after the fleece God allowed Gideon and his friend to go into the camp of the Midianites and hear the prophecy from the man who spoke of " . . . the sword of the Lord and of Gideon . . . " (Judges 7:14) So if I have a challenge for you in this expendable devotional it is to like the disciples of Jesus pray: " . . . Increase our faith . . . " (Luke 17:5) Let us never speak poorly of 'fleece faith', but let us never be satisfied with it either. It is just one of the first steps on the ladder of faith that ought to grow and mature as we grow and mature in our understanding of our God. "Fleece faith' is one of the building blocks of faith " . . . when your faith is increased . . . " (II Corinthians 10:15) If your faith has increased over time and you look back on your history of faith you will recognize the importance of that first faith, like Gideon's 'fleece faith'; not expendable!

46

Tabitha—The Special Seamstress

Acts 9:40

And Peter put them all forth, and kneeling down, and prayed: and turning him to the body said, Tabitha, arise. And she opened her eyes: and when she saw Peter, she sat up.

WHAT DO YOU CONSIDER GOD'S work? For most of us it has to be teaching God's Word, or preaching God's Gospel, or evangelizing God's people; these are certainly at the top aren't they? If you're right and the majority of the church thinks so; then where would you put sewing? I hope after you consider this 'expendable' story from the Scriptures that you will have reconsidered its placement near the top of your list. If this is what transpires then it will all happen because of a little known, early believer by the name of Tabitha, or Dorcas.

It was the custom of those days for Jewish people in Gentile controlled Canaan, or Palestine to be given two names: one Hebrew and one Greek. At the time of this story Joppa was both a Gentile town and a Jewish village. Despite the seemingly difference between the two names; Tabitha and Dorcas, both actually mean the same: 'gazelle, with Tabitha being the Hebrew name and Dorcas being the Greek name. In the East, this name was a popular name given to baby girls because the indication is 'as beautiful as a deer' (Song of Solomon 2:9, 17, 4:5, 9:3). Was Tabitha's beauty an outward one or an inward one, or both? I like the way this writer put it in writing of Tabitha:

Tabitha—the Special Seamstress

"It suited her well, for she was not only swift to run errands of mercy, but she performed her good works so gracefully that those who were benefited by them loved her dearly. Her faithful devotion to the Saviour in commonplace things and her compassion for her friends and neighbors made her a model Christian!" And could I simply add: not expendable, indispensible!

The tender story of Tabitha is recorded in Acts 9:36–42, and it brings to light a ministry that is almost extent today, and that is in ministering to the needy, a help in areas in which others can't but you can. This is the only place Tabitha is mention in the written Word, but unlike so many before and after at least her story is mentioned and she is not an unnamed, unknown Christian. In this age of nursing homes, boarding homes, and governmental agencies for the aged, the ministry of ministering to the needy has been dropped in the lap of government. It was not always that way! Most Church members as well as family member who have a needy person in their midst has long ago deposited that church member, family member into some social day care, or nightly care center and has long forgotten their responsibility. But in the days of Tabitha there were no such organizations; there was the Church and in the Church there was Tabitha. I have been ministering in boarding home and nursing homes and special care homes for over fifty years (1970–2020) at the writing of this devotional and I have wondered for years who could do the better job for caring. Tabitha's specialty were the widows of the region and in particular their clothing: "This woman was full of good works and almsdeeds which she did." (Acts 9:36) If you needed a dress or a pair of pants fixed she would do it, but the language that Luke uses in the description of Tabitha's work suggests she was best at making under-coats and outer-garments for the widows and the needy. Tabitha was Job-like: "If I have seen any perish for want of clothing or nay poor without covering; if his loins have not blessed men, and if he were not warmed with the fleece of my sheep." (Job 31:19–20) Tabitha was a seamstress for her Saviour!

An attitude of helping the needy is encouraged in the Law of Moses wherein the farmer is instructed: "When ye reap the harvest of your land, thou shalt not wholly reap the corners of the field." (Leviticus 19:9) The main part of the field could be rightfully claimed by the sower, the owner, but the margins, the corners were to be set aside for the needy and stranger passing through, but if you are a seamstress and not a sower, does this precept still apply to you? To say: "I would like to help!" is an empty benevolence. A hollow-hand of help is little help to the needy. I like Phillips translation of James 2:15-16: "If a fellow man or woman has no clothes to wear and nothing to eat, and one of you say, Good luck to you, I hope you'll keep warm and find enough to eat, and yet give them nothing to meet their physical needs, what on earth is the good of that?" Tabitha had no such attitude! I am reminded of Jesus' classic story of the prodigal in the far country when he was in need " . . . no one gave him anything . . . " (Luke 15:16 Moffatt) Someone has interestingly asked: "If the Christian Gospel had reached the people of that country, would they have cared for him?" A simple reading of Jesus instructions of Matthew 25:35-40 will reveal that " . . . naked, and ye clothed me . . . " was enough for Tabitha!

Such ministries are out of sight, behind the scenes and if not for the untimely death of Tabitha we might never have known of this extraordinary life and work. Probably her good words and alms deeds to the citizens of Joppa never made the local paper, or the nightly news, the Christians of Joppa were so overcome they didn't believe they could go on without Tabitha, so they called for Peter. Over my nearly 48 years in the pastorate I too have discovered that most local churches can replace a deacon, a Sunday school teacher, and yes, even a pastor, but few churches can replace people like Tabitha. Recently, I have been confronted again with the marvellous teaching of Paul concerning 'the spiritual gifts' in I Corinthians 12. Most don't even see Tabitha's gift unless you look carefully. Only mentioned once and its description in only one five letter word, few see it, recognize it, most simply pass over it, but for me it is one of the most important gifts given to the Church: 'helps' (I Corinthians 12:28). Tabitha had it and the church needed it and the Church wanted Tabitha back with it!

Many Christians aspired to the lofty positions in church work, but few volunteer for the 'needy' ministries. Have we become so far removed from the earliest example of the Church in Jerusalem that we have forgotten that the very first official business the Church ever undertook after evangelism was the care of the widows, the needy (Acts 6:1-3). The Bible says that Peter arrived at Joppa and dismissed all the mourners from the room where Tabitha was layed. Then simply following the example of Jesus at the resurrection of Jarius' daughter (remember Peter was there-Matthew 9:23-25), Peter raised Tabitha up through the Power of the Holy Spirit: " . . . and gave her hand and lifted her up and he called the saints and the widows, presented her alive." (Acts 9:41) This humble servant was given back to the local assembly to continue doing the vital work of caring for the widows. Surely we have come to the place where we realize that it is not what we get but give that is important to the work of the Lord. So many, so many even in the Church are only out to make living verses making a difference. So no matter what skill you have, even the skill of a needle, it can be used for the glory of the Saviour and the need of the Church: for God's glory and the widow's good.

47

Abiathar—The Sole Survivor

I Samuel 22:20

And one of the sons of Ahimelech the son of Ahitub, named Abiathar, escaped, and fled to David.

I am convinced that 'remnant theology' is an important Biblical doctrine being ignored today. Rooted in the Old Testament belief, this orthodox teaching was prompted by Jews theologians to help combat paganism and its attempt to made inroads into the Jew's faith. This theology was necessary especially in the 'captivities' (Assyrian and Babylonian) as there were those that taught that God had forsaken His people; "remnant" theology stresses that God will always preserve a faithful remnant (those faithful just to Him) in every generation, so that 'the faith' might survive. I do believe an insightful study of the Old Testament will reveal that this is a genuine interpretation of what God did in relationship to Israel. In ever age, no matter how difficult or apostate, God protected and preserved certain individuals and groups of Jews in their faith. God always had a few, if not many, who remain loyal and obedient to His Word and His ways. While others fell away and departed from the faith, others stayed true and dedicated to preserving the Jew's form of worship and living. I believe a case in point to this way of seeing God work is mentioned in the verse I have given you to start this 'expendable' devotional; a solo survivor that illustrates and underlines the teaching of 'remnant theology, and what God considers 'expendable'!

Abiathar—the Sole Survivor

Abiathar might not be as famous as Aaron, but they did have something in common. Both were named to the highest office of the Jewish religion and the Levitical worship system. Abiathar attained that lofty office by the infamous death of his father. During the days of Israel's first king, Saul, the High Priest was a man by the name of Ahimelech, the son of Ahitub, a descendent of the High Priest Eli (I Samuel 1–4). Ahimelech and Abiathar, with other priests lived in a place called Nob, a small village just a few miles from Mount Moriah. When I travelled to Jerusalem in 2010, we could see Nob from the rampart wall. All told there were 85 priests in Nob in Saul's day, all who wore the '. . . linen ephod . . .' (I Samuel 22:18) Joshua had established (Joshua 18:1) the tabernacle at Shiloh (another site I got to visit in 2010), but after the defeat of the Israelites in Eben-Ezar (I Samuel 4:1) Shiloh was presumably destroyed by the Philistines and the priests were scattered. The Ark of the Covenant, which had been captures, eventually settled in the house of Abinadad (I Samuel 7:1) until David finally moved it to Jerusalem during the first years of his reign (II Samuel 6). Sometime in the meantime this group of priests had found their way to Nob and had established a community of priests there. The village was known as " . . . a city of priests . . . " (I Samuel 22:19).

In the list of the settlements at the return of the Jews from the Babylonian Captivity (Nehemiah 11:32), Nob was located between Anathoth and Ananiah. This put Nob in the tribal territory of Benjamin, not far from Saul's capital of Gibeah (another site I was able to visit in our May 2010 trip to Israel). Historically, Nob was the high water mark for Sennacherib's advance into Judah in the days of Hezekiah: "This very day he will halt at Nob, he will shake his fist at the mount of the daughter of Zion, the hill of Jerusalem." (Isaiah 10:32). If I could see Nob from Jerusalem then the Assyrian king could see Jerusalem from Nob! But for all of Nob's history it will forever be remembered for the infamous day that one man (Doeg the Edomite) slaughtered, massacred 84 men of God, and a young man by the name of Abiathar was the sole survivor from this unprovoked attack and tragic incident at Nob.

Abiathar's father had helped David escape from King Saul by giving him bread (I Samuel 21:6) and the sword of Goliath (I Samuel 21:9) which had been kept as a symbol of God's great victory over the giant at the Battle of Elah (I Samuel 17). However, David had been spotted at Nob by a servant of Saul's by the name of Doeg. As of the growth of Saul's properties and position, Saul was obligated to appoint ministers over his affairs; thus Doeg the Edomite was "... chief of Saul's herdsmen..." (I Samuel 22:9) Because David was public enemy number one in Saul's realm and to demonstrate his loyalty, Doeg informed the king of David's presence, so close to Gibeah! Saul was so furious that David had been so close and that the priests had not turned him in that he demanded their deaths. Saul's own men wouldn't raise a hand against the Lord's priests, but Doeg did the dirt work and killed 84 of 85. By the grace of God and the doctrine of the remnant, Abiathar escapes only to find refuge in David's camp: "Abide thou with me, fear not: for he that seeketh my life seeketh thy life: but with me thou shalt be in safeguard." (I Samuel 22:33) Why do some die and some live in a terrorist attack? Despite the almost daily terrorist attacks happening today around the world we must remember that God is still in control of who dies and who lives. As I write this devotional the terrible slaughter in a small Texas church is on my mind. We are stocked, but Nob massacres have been happening for thousands of years now. The truth we must see is that whether in Texas or Israel God will provide a way of escape to any person who is a part of God's divine remnant: people like Abiathar.

After Abiathar's near death experience, he became a close friend and spiritual advisor to David through the bulk of David's life. This relationship was done through one thing that had escaped Nob with Abiathar-the ephod: "And it came to pass, when Abiathar the son of Ahimelech fled to David to Keilah that he came down with the ephod in his hand." (I Samuel 23:6) Connected to the sacred Jewish Ephod was the "Urim and the Thummim" (Exodus 28:30) those mysterious, special stones that were used by the priests to seek God's will in certain affairs. During David's dilemma over the capture of his family in Ziklag, he asked Abiathar to bring the Ephod before the Lord to seek God's direction whether he ought to chase the Amalekites or not (I Samuel 30:7)? Abiathar played a significant role during David's years as a guerrilla leader. Despite living from cave to cave, Abiathar stayed loyal to David through the tough year; a man David needed and the reason in my opinion why Abiathar survived Nob, another one of God's remnant.

I believe the 'theology of the remnant' is also found in the New Testament teachings of Paul. The great Apostle writes this in his letter to the Romans: "Even so then at this present time also there is a remnant according to the election of grace." (Romans 11:5) There are those that don't believe this is speaking about the Jews but the Church. I will disagree because the Church is far from a remnant, or the need of remnant theology throughout its history. Granted, the Lord will always have His witness, and He will

Abiathar—The Sole Survivor

always 'save some' in each generation, in each nation, but Abiathar was a Jew and Paul recognized God's amazing hand of grace on his nation. For me I believe it is one of the missions of the Church to rise up a remnant both in the Gentile world and the Jewish world. We are left with the task of sharing Christ with both Jew and Gentile and though a family might be lost one can be saved. Though a race might be lost a sole survivor will be heard around the Throne of God praising Him for eternity (Revelation 5:9 and 7:9)!

48

MEBUNNAI—THE TREMENDOUS TROOPER

II SAMUEL 23:27

Abiezer the Anethothite, **MEBUNNAI** the Hushathite.

COMPARING DAVID'S LISTINGS OF HIS 'mighty men' in II Samuel 23 and I Chronicles 11, the next warrior in order would be a man by the name of Mebunnai, or Sibbecai. I have come to believe these two names are for the same soldier because they fall in the same slot or the same order David gave them in II Samuel 23, and the same order recorded in I Chronicles 11. They both are called Hushathites, the patronymic of the family of Hushah of the tribe of Judah (I Chronicles 4:4), and this is all we know for sure about this mighty man of David:

1. Mebunnai: "the eighth captain for the eighth month was Sibbecai the Hushathites of the Zarhites (from Zarah or Zerah, the son of Judah-Numbers 26:20) and in his course were twenty and four thousand." (I Chronicles 27:11) This would have made Mebunnai one of David top dozen generals, responsible for a month of the years in the protection of the borders of Israel!

2. Mebunnai is also recorded as the man who killed a 'giant': "And it came to pass after this, that there was again a battle with the Philistines at Gob: then Sibbechai (Sibbecai) the Hushathite slew Saph (possibly a brother to Goliath), which was one of the sons of the giant." (II Samuel 21:18 and I Chronicles 20:4) Mebunnai's only call to Biblical

fame was at the second Battle at Gob when he took on the giant Saph and killed him, but that event was enough to immortalize Mebunnai in the Word of God. We know very little of this battle; we don't even know how Mebunnai slew Saph, but perhaps that is the way the Lord wanted us to remember Mebunnai. I believe Mebunnai was just one of David's ordinary soldiers at the Battle of Gob, but before the battle was over Mebunnai would go down in Jewish history as a 'giant-killer'! Will we stand in this evil day against the giants that still stalk the land? These giants might not be gigantic in size but in intellect, in position, in power whose 'every imagination of the thoughts of the heart was (is) only evil continually." (Genesis 6:5) In the days of Noah they were called 'men of renown', and Jesus warned us that as the days of Noah so would the coming of the Son of God be (Matthew 24:37); for me this includes 'giants'. We too must develop our fighting skills, so like Mebunnai we might take on the 'giants'!

3. Sibbecai means 'Jehovah is intervening', but Mebunnai means 'built up', and it is around that name and meaning I would like to challenge you from this verse in Colossians 2:7: "Rooted and BUILT UP in Him, and stablished in the faith, as ye have been taught, abounding with thanksgiving." As Mebunnai helped David built up the nation of Israel after the civil war with the family of Saul and the countless wars with the enemies that surrounded Israel, so too must we learn to 'built up'!

If there is anybody that is expendable it is the warrior, the soldier, the man who puts his life on the line every time he steps out onto the battlefield.

Dave Egner, writing in an Our Daily Bread article, a publication of the Radio Bible Class, once recorded this: "Scripture portrays the Christian life as a process of growth in which we advance from one stage to the next: from spiritual infancy to maturity, from milk to strong meat, from being rooted in Christ to being firmly established. We may want to be grown up all at once, but we must learn to take one step at a time. I realized this anew as my 16-month-old granddaughter and I were walking along the channel in Muskegon, Michigan. I was in somewhat of a hurry, but Kelsey was not. From her toddler perspective, she had seen a 6-inch-ledge that ran the length of the walkway. Slowly and carefully she climbed on top of the ledge. After standing there triumphantly for a moment, she cautiously stepped back down. It was quite an accomplishment for the little tyke. Then she wanted to make sure she mastered it well. So she a few feet farther down the walk climbed onto the ledge again. I patiently waited for her because I knew this was an important phase of her learning. And I thought, I can learn from her. I need to be sure I've mastered one spiritual discipline before proceeding to one that is more advanced. Then I won't become discouraged in my climb to maturity. Spiritual growth occur a step at a time." One of the dangers often repeated in the Bible (I Corinthians 3:1-3-Hebrews 5:11-14) is the scourge of spiritual stagnation; when the believer doesn't grow but stays the same. We might start out with milk (I Peter 2:2), but we need to grow into strong meat (Hebrews 5:14)! This happens when we are 'built up' in Christ feeding daily on this word (II Peter 3:18).

Christ said, "I will build my Church." (Matthew 16:18) As Dave Egner watched his granddaughter expand her abilities and boundaries, so too does Christ watch us as we walk through this life. Mr. Egner saw a tiny glimpse of the advancement of his granddaughter during their walk together along that channel in Michigan, so too does Christ see us being built up in Him, even though, like the little girl, we never notice it ourselves. Ours is an observation that is made over time as we realize that we are not the same, our interests are not the same over time. Christ has the ability to see our slightest advancements, or steps enlarging, or interests expanding: growing up is built up! Peter makes an interesting analogy to this concept in his first epistle to the scattered saints (I Peter 1:1). After speaking of the newborn (I Peter 2:2), he speaks of the saints as 'lively stones' being built up as a spiritual house (I Peter 2:5). Ethel Barrett, in her book (It Only Hurts When I Laugh-Regal Books-1973) tells the story of the king of Sparta and his boast to a Greek ambassador of the invincible walls of Sparta. The visitor quickly asked if he might see these walls. The king's reply was that in the morning the Greek ambassador would be taken on a tour of the walls of Sparta. The next morning, to the ambassador's surprise, the king of Sparta took his guest through the gates of the city onto the plains outside the town. Their standing in perfect order and attention was the well-disciplined and world-famous army of Sparta. The king of Sparta pointed to his troops and proclaimed: "There they are! There are the walls of Sparta!" I have come to believe that we too are to be such walls. In the New Testament the Church of Christ is likened to a bride (Ephesians 5), a brotherhood (I Peter 2:17), a body (I Corinthians 12), but also a building (Ephesians 2:21-22). As we speak the Good Lord through His Spirit is building up His 'temple', a temple not made with brick and granite, timber or tile, but 'lively stones', you and me, so as we are built up we are being built in to the building of God!

Believer by believer, Christ too is building up His Church. Has He put you into His building yet? Have you been built up into God's walls yet? If you haven't, my encouragement to you would be to yield to the Master bricklayer, and let him use you to finish His wall (work)! Mebunnai is a good example to us through the meaning of his name, but his other name is just as important (Jehovah is intervening). Only when the Father choses the stone, and only when the Spirit convicts (prepares) the stone, while Jesus be able to take that stone and make it apart of His grand building: the Church. In order to be a piece of Christ's building we must be willing to be expendable to the cause.

49

Nathan—The Straightforward Seer

II Samuel 12:1

And the Lord send Nathan unto David. And he came unto him, and said unto him, there were two men in one city; the one rich, and the other poor.

I HAVE COME TO BELIEVE that the seer Nathan was chosen of God to step into the shoes of the departed Samuel. After God determined that Israel would be governed by kings instead of judges (a 450 year period-Acts 13:20), there was still the need for a direct communication with the Almighty, a spokesman who could tell the kings what God wanted them to do, and for most of the kingship of King Saul Samuel was that man, but in the kingship of David, Nathan was the spokesman for God. As in the life of Samuel, so in the life of Nathan sometimes the seer had to deliver a difficult message and every time they did they put their lives on the line; they were expendable but the message wasn't!

    Nathan is first mentioned in the Bible as advising David concerning David's desire to build a sanctuary for the Ark of the Covenant (II Samuel 7:2). At first Nathan advised the king to " **. . . Go, do all that is in thine heart; for the Lord is with thee.**" (II Samuel 7:3) Or so Nathan thought; it seemed to be a no-brainer, why wouldn't God want a Temple built in His honor? But Nathan was wrong because he failed to ask God about it before advising David! I have wondered if most of the grandiose construction projects throughout history and even now in the name of the Lord are wrong. The hours spent and the money spent could be used in other God ordained ventures. Like Nathan we forget to ask God what He thinks about our schemes in His name; especially in the building of chapels and cathedrals and churches that build on our pride more than His presence. Have we forgotten what Jesus said to the woman at the well? "Women, believe me, the hour cometh when ye shall neither in this mountain, nor yet in Jerusalem, worship the Father . . . but the hour cometh, and now is, when the true worshippers shall worship the Father in spirit and in truth, for the Father seeketh such to worship Him." (John 4:21, 23) It wasn't until the third century that the Church had it first church building, and then in the days of Constantine a fixation and a fascination with buildings really began. Nathan was wrong then and we are wrong now, but few see such buildings as expendable!

So the same day Nathan advised David to build, he was visited by the Lord telling him to tell David differently. How embarrassing that conversation must have been? Construction was to stop immediately, but the gathering of materials and engineering of the Temple would continue. It isn't that God didn't want a Temple, but God's timing and God's man was David's son Solomon (II Samuel 7:4–17). He would get the honor and privilege of construction God's Temple on Mount Moriah (II Chronicles 3:1) not David. I don't think God is against our houses of worship, but we need to be careful we don't misunderstand their purpose. What Nathan didn't understand the timing wasn't right for the construction of God's house because David was a man of war and the borders hadn't been secured? God wanted his building to be a building of peace (I Chronicles 22:9). It is a difficult job to deliver a message of "no", but brave men like Nathan are not stopped when it comes to God's tough decrees; they are not expendable!

The second and most famous interview between David and Nathan occurred about a year after the king's adulterous affair with the beauty Bathsheba and the murder of the lady's war-hero husband Uriah. This time Nathan didn't approach the king as an advisor but an accuser. It is one thing to say 'no' to a man's heartfelt desire to please his God, but it takes a special courage and a fearless countenance to expose a man's secret and hideous sin; especially when you are going up against the most powerful man in the land. John the Baptist learned just how dangerous this prospect could be when he proclaimed to King Herod and his adulterous mistress Herodias: " . . . It is not lawful for thee to have her . . . " (Matthew 14:4)

Condemning Herod's marriage to his brother's wife eventually cost John his head, expendable! But such was Nathan's dilemma, commission, to expose the king's wicked sins. Perhaps, the most famous words ever spoken by this straightforward seer were: "**. . . Thou art that man . . .** " (II Samuel 12:7)

Nathan's words, unlike John the Baptist's words, were enough however to turn David's heart around. The compiler of the Psalms makes an interesting comment just before quoting David's psalm he numbered "Fifty-One": "To the chief musicians, a psalm of David, when Nathan the prophet came unto him, after he had gone in to Bathsheba." Perhaps, the best example of true repentance came about because Nathan was willing to face the wrath of the king. Let us never forget that we are not helping our friends or a family member by helping them cover up a sin! Though Nathan didn't know this precept from the pen of Paul he practiced it: **"Brethren, if a man be overtaken in a fault, ye which are spiritual, restore such an one in the spirit of meekness; considering thyself, lest thee also be tempted."** (Galatians 6:1) The best thing Nathan ever did for David was helping him come face to face with his wickedness. To reveal the evil of any sin is always the best policy. Do you have the moral courage to speak boldly to those you love about their sin? It is tough to do, but it is the best thing to do!

Our friendships and relationships are expendable to the revealing of sins and transgressions that will eventually destroy our friendship and relationship if they are not exposed and dealt with. Can you imagine what David's and Nathan's relationship would have been after Nathan found out about the affair and had kept silent about it? Jesus confronted His disciples James and John with a sinful trait in their lives when he called them " . . . sons of thunder . . . " (Mark 3:17) They were tough, tempestuous fishermen from the Sea of Galilee. The life style had made them hard, uncompassionate and early in their relationship the brothers were found to be harsh and merciless. On one occasion John saw a man casting out devils in the name of the Lord, but the man wasn't one of the disciples, so John took it upon himself to rebuke the man. (Luke 10:49–50) Jesus in turn rebuked John for his attribute; how the so-called 'fighting fundamentalists' need this admonition today! On another occasion Jesus was not invited or welcomed into a certain Samaritan village and the brothers in unison asked Jesus permission to call fire from heaven to consume the entire town, like Sodom! Once again Jesus had to confront His closest disciples and rebuke them for their suggestion (Luke 10:52–56). Despite these negative characteristics Jesus over the years of His development of his disciples transformed the brothers to the place that John would be eventually known as 'the apostle of love'. (You need to read John's first epistle to realize this transformation!)

James and John needed Jesus' confrontations and David needed Nathan's spiritual rebuke through the simple parable of the rich man and the poor man. David's deadly flaw needed correction if he was to continue on as king. What was true of Jesus and Nathan is also true for us. We need to monitor the situations and circumstance our family and friends get themselves into. Unlike Cain belief, we are called on to be our brother's keeper, and if we aren't willing to put our relationship on the line to correct them, then what you see as expendable is the purity of the body and the holiness of the soul!

50

Esau—The Despising Delinquent

Genesis 25:34

Then Jacob gave Esau bread and pottage of lentils; and he did eat and drink, and rose up, and went his way: thus Esau despised his birthright.

MANY PEOPLE OVER THE YEARS have been upset with God's statement about Esau in the prophetic book of Malachi (Malachi 1:2) and quoted again by the Apostle Paul in his letter to the Romans **"As it is written, Jacob have I loved, but Esau have I hated."** (Romans 9:13). Some have even claimed this this is a direct contradiction of Jesus classic statement: "For God so loved the world that He gave His only begotten son that whosoever believeth in Him shall not perish but have everlasting life." (John 3:16) Yet I have come to the same conclusion as Paul on this issue: "What shall we say then? Is there unrighteousness with God? God forbid!" (Romans 9:14) You have heard it said of pastors and missionaries for years: <u>**"God loves the sinner, but hates the sin!"**</u> What was it about the man Esau that brought such hatred for him by God Himself? I have come to the conclusion it all has to do with what Esau saw as expendable and what God saw as not being expendable. What Esau saw as unimportant and what God saw as important. Esau got his 'expendables' mixed up, as we often do.

The patriarchs of Israel practiced the Middle East custom of the 'birthright', which gave special favor to the son that was born first in the family. Even though Esau and Jacob were twins, Esau was born first making

Esau—the Despising Delinquent

him the oldest son of Isaac. (Genesis 25:25) In Bible times the first born son would get a double portion of his father's goods when the father died, and he would also be appointed the head of the clan and ruler over all that the father owned. He would have power over the bulk of the father's property which included widows, unmarried daughters, and younger sons, like Jacob. I found an interesting custom in India that seems to reverse this order when in Kerala State it is the youngest son that is ultimately responsible for the care of the father's estate when he dies! However, the birthright could be taken away in cases of terrible transgressions as was the case of Reuben, Jacob's oldest son, (Genesis 49:3–4) when Reuben committed the iniquity of sleeping with one of Jacob's concubines! The birthright could also be traded or given away as Esau did. When we see something worth trading, we see the thing to be traded as expendable; not as valuable or important as the thing we are trading for! Reuben saw his 'love' or was it lust with his stepmother more important than his birthright, or was he just jumping the gun and assuming his right of the birthright prematurely? (Think this act of wickedness not strange for there was a man in the Corinthian Church that did the same thing-I Corinthians 5:1) Judas saw thirty pieces of silver more valuable that his relationship with Jesus Christ. Jesus was expendable to Judas and Esau's birthright was expendable to him!

Esau was a man who loved the out-of-doors, not the indoors of a tent (Genesis 25:27). Esau loved the freedom of the open spaces, the hunt, and he cared not for the responsibilities of property or people. Esau loved to do what Esau loved to do, and he didn't want to be confined to any rules and regulations, house or home, and I have come to believe the responsibilities of being head of a family and with that the spiritual leader of the clan; in other words Esau didn't believe in his father's God as Jacob would! Jacob on the other hand was just the opposite of Esau; as is often the case with brothers or children. My two kids were polar opposites in every way! Jacob wanted control, order. Jacob wanted to be in charge; Jacob wanted Esau's birthright, so on the day that Esau came up empty on his daily hunt, Jacob saw the opportunity he was looking for. In the spur of the moment Esau thought only of his stomach and was persuaded by Jacob to sell his birthright for a cup of soup (Genesis 25:29–33). Probably next to the purchase of Manhattan from the Indians for a few trinkets or Alaska from the Russians for a few bucks there has been no more lopsided transition in history than this! Isaac was one of the wealthiest men in Palestine and a deed from God for all of Canaan, yet "Esau despised his birthright." (Genesis 25:34) I have come to believe this despising included God Himself, so Esau's family's inheritance was expendable but his appetite was not?

With the birthright came the father's blessing (Genesis 27:4) which meant the father would pass on to his son God's favor. By the time Esau grew-up enough to understand the importance of the birthright he wanted the blessing, but like Cain and Abel, Esau and Jacob saw God differently. One can build a case even from the Bible that in most affairs Esau was the more noble, but God looks at the heart (I Samuel 16:7). God saw that Esau was far from him that he would never really worship Him, and though Jacob played the fool most of his life, but in the end Jacob would trust and love the God of Abraham and Isaac as they did! Jacob like the prodigal son (Luke 15:11–32) would leave home a rebel and Esau would like the older son stay home, yet in the end it was Jacob who become Israel and Esau became the bitter older son! Even when we seemingly say the right things, do the right things and play the right part our hearts can be far from God and He knows it. With the birthright and the blessing came the spiritual headship of the family and though Jacob was the juvenile delinquent, Esau would be the despising delinquent!

The birthright and the blessing were really Jacob's from the very beginning as was told to their mother before their birth (Genesis 25:23). How was this possible? Paul wrote: **"For whom He did foreknow, He also did predestinate to be conformed to the image of His Son . . . "** (Romans 8:29) God loves us and hates us on His foreknowledge of our love or hate for Him. Paul would also write: **"For He saith to Moses, I will have mercy on whom I will have mercy, and I will have compassion on whom I will have compassion."** (Romans 9:15) Now that we know 'the rest of the story' we can clearly see what God saw in both Jacob and Esau. We sometimes get upset with God because we don't see the whole picture, but when we do we discover that God was right all along. That Jacob would worship the True and Living God, and Esau would worship other gods.

What was true in the life of Esau is seen again in the life of the king of Egypt. A careful reading of the life of Pharaoh in the days of the Exodus reveals that Pharaoh was just playing for time and when it says that God's hardened Pharaoh's heart it was Pharaoh who first hardened his heart! (Exodus 7–13) Even when Pharaoh eventually let the Israelites go he still went after them until the Red Sea disaster. Pharaoh's heart was already hardened toward God and so was Esau's heart. He did some wonderful things like forgiving his brother of all his deception and deceit, but in the end he was not the man to bring a Messiah into the world through. Such men are not predetermined they are just determined to set their own course, do it their way, establish their own standards of the value of things. What God seems as important they see as unimportant, what God puts value too they see as invaluable. What God sees as treasure men like Esau and Pharaoh see as trash? In the end Esau make the wrong evaluation of what was important, what was expendable and what wasn't (II Corinthians 4:18) and each of us must choose: expendable or eternal which will we choose? Esau choose wrong Jacob choose right!

Postlude

Hebrews 11:32

And what shall I more say? For time would fail me to tell of . . .

MORE OFTEN THAN NOT WHEN I near the end of a writing project, I feel like the Apostle Paul as he was wrapping up one of the great chapter of the Bible: Hebrews 11-the hall of the faithful. Heroes and heroines he wrote about, as one by one he listed the great examples of faith in the Old Testament, and despite the lengthy list there were others; those he didn't have time for " . . . Gedeon, and of Barak, and of Samson, and of Jephthae; of David also, and Samuel, and of the prophets." (Hebrews 11:32) How many expendable stories were there in the compiling of the Scriptures? But unlike the broad description Paul gave for those he couldn't specifically write of (Hebrews 11:33-40), I am going to give you one more, one more Biblical character that highlights and underline again the scriptural doctrine of 'expandable'; I would like for you to meet Ehud, one of the special deliverers the Lord God raised up to deliver the children of Israel in a time of trial (Judges 3:15), a mighty man of God that knew about expendability!

God has the amazing ability to have the right man prepared for the right task while being in the right place to do that which is right. We know of the more famous Esther who according to her uncle " . . . **and who knoweth, whether thou art come to the kingdom for such a time as this?**" (Esther 4:14) But have you ever considered Ehud in light of this divine providential precept? The left-handed Benjamite who become God's righthand man during the Moabite occupation; a man who saw his life as expendable for God and God's mission, but who God saw as valuable to the cause. When will we realize that life and one's work is valuable to God even

POSTLUDE

when He seems to put our lives on the line for that work? Ehud was not the first as we have seen and Ehud wasn't the last as we have seen, but neither are we. We are but one in a long list of those God has called to make the ultimate sacrifice (Rom. 12:1); even when we don't have to ultimately make it!

Fat King Eglon (Judges 3:17) had occupied Israel with a ten-thousand man expeditionary force of might men for eighteen years (Judges 3:14, 24). The children of Israel eventually cried unto the Lord for help (Judges 3:15) and deliverance from the oppression. (We should never forget that Israel had brought this chastisement upon themselves because of their worship of the 'gods' of the land, but every time the Hebrew would repent God would answer!) In answer to their prayer God called on Ehud to answer their prayer, as God often does. **God can use you to answer a prayer!** I believe that God is always in the process of preparing for His children's deliverance. Did He not started before the foundation of the world for our redemption (I Peter 1:19–20)? Even before we get into trouble God is at work preparing for our need. Because people are God's preferred method of salvation, God was rising up a young man through those years of oppression whose dominate hand was his left-hand. Have you ever wondered why God makes right-handed and left-handed people? Ehud grew to be " . . . a man left-handed . . . " (Judges 3:13) Why? God knew why because one day Ehud's left-hand would be the key to a victory over the Moabites. What special traits has God put in you for some future event? And remember, there is no such thing as a useless member of your body, or the Body of Christ! (I Corinthians 12:22–24) For Ehud it was his left-hand and the knife (Judges 3:16) that he would handle in a very unique and unusual way!

Where men see problems, an obstacle, God sees possibilities. I believe it was the Almighty who inspired Ehud to use his natural ability and his favorite weapon to start a revolt against the occupiers. Most people now and then are right-handed. So when Ehud walked through security at Eglon's palace in Jericho (Judges 3:17–18) the guards only patted down his left side, the normal side for carrying a weapon. Ehud had proven to himself that he could get through Eglon's defensives with a weapon. Because Ehud had brought the annual tribute before without incident the guards were lack and Eglon seeming didn't fear the young Hebrew. On the appointed time Ehud once again delivered the taxes, but this time he made sure those who were with him left (Judges 3:19), but he would stay and deliver the assassin's blow himself. Some would call this a suicide mission with no means of escape, yet Ehud had planned well. Granted, Ehud saw himself as expendable, but he still planned an escape. What do you do when God calls you to a seemingly impossible mission; are you willing to forsake all, lay all on the altar, and surrender all to its accomplishment? (Luke 14:16–20) Are you willing to be expendable?

Successfully slipping through security for a second time Ehud was able to convince King Eglon into a private meeting (Judges 3:20). When alone with the king in his upper chamber and the door barred Ehud struck a blow for freedom from the Moabite tyranny by killing the king (Judges 3:21–22). Having locked the doors to the room allowed Ehud to escape out a back window long before the Moabite guards realized what had happened (Judges 3:23–25). When the news spread throughout the land that the evil king was died, the Jews began to rally behind their newest hero (Judges 3:30). And as they say the rest is history. All because a young man had the moral courage to take a stand against evil and all because he believed his life was expendable but the life of his nation wasn't. Every generation is looking for the 'one' who is willing to put it all on the line to resist the evil of the day. Today we face many wicked men who seemingly are occupying what is not rightfully theirs but they set fat and happy in their ivory palaces feasting on the tribute they inflict on the masses. Expendable Ehuds are what we need!

Do people call you backward because of some physical difference? Has God made you just a bit different than most folks? Maybe He has raised you up with such abilities or lack of abilities (I Corinthians 1:26–29) so that you might accomplish something only you can accomplish. Do you see your left-hand as an asset or a liability? When I was much younger than I am today there was a brilliant one-handed pitcher by the name of Jim Abbott who accomplished the greatest feat for a pitcher and that being a no-hitter in the major leagues. I have come to believe the question isn't if God can use you for something special, but the question is do you want to be used for something special? Are you willing to put what you have on the line; who you are on the line, are you willing to go into the devil's lair and face him down surrounded by his demons? Expendable, but remember God will also make a way of escape (I Corinthians 10:13).

I will leave the rest of the 'expendable' characters of the Bible for your discovery, but I leave you with this final challenge from Jesus: **"For whosoever will save his life shall lose it: and whosoever will lose his life for my sake shall fine it."** (Matthew 16:25) My paraphrase of this classic verse goes

POSTLUDE

something like this: "For those of us who will not see our lives as 'expendable' will ultimately fail, but those of us who will count our lives as 'expendable' will never, ever know defeat!"

Barry Blackstone
July 2021

www.ingramcontent.com/pod-product-compliance
Lightning Source LLC
Chambersburg PA
CBHW071441150426
43191CB00008B/1190